The Fantastic Art of Rowena

Foreword by
Theodore Sturgeon

Introduction by
Boris Vallejo

PUBLISHED BY POCKET BOOKS NEW YORK

Another *Original* publication of POCKET BOOKS

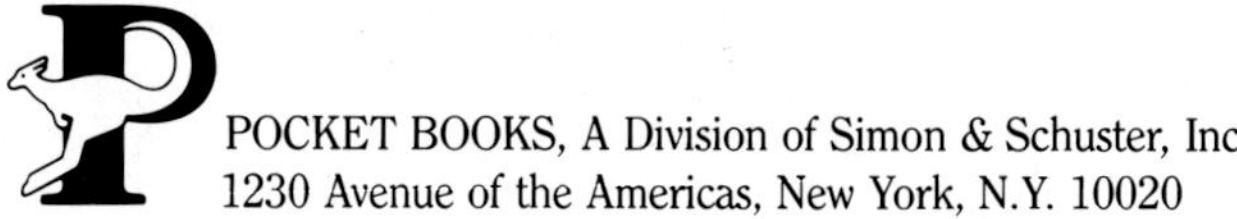

POCKET BOOKS, A Division of Simon & Schuster, Inc.
1230 Avenue of the Americas, New York, N.Y. 10020

ISBN: 0-671-47055-8

First Pocket Books printing September, 1983

10 9 8 7 6 5 4 3 2 1

The Fantastic Art of Rowena

Introduction

When I met Rowena for the first time, I was struck immediately by the delicacy of her appearance, the soft careful modulation of her voice, and the reserved manner which, for me, was somewhat incongruous with the composer of such eerily humorous and visually exciting paintings as *Twilight Terrors*, with its touchingly brave little boy and jewel-like but quite convincingly frightening monster, and *Who Fears the Devil*, with its exquisitely nightmarish creatures.

While it is true that a commercial illustrator must follow, to a degree, the manuscript that is being illustrated, I have always felt that art is an explicit extension, however subtle, of the artist; the worlds that have been shaped on the canvas are directly linked with the artist's inner world.

So this is Rowena, I thought. I had originally visualized her as being six feet tall, like one of the more heroic females of her paintings. (In fact, she is indeed the model for some of the women in her work.) As I got to know her better, I realized that behind her quiet reserve were an iron will and a Spartan determination to work as hard as necessary to achieve her goals.

When Rowena spoke about her first art class, she recounted the difficulty she had experienced in composing a still life. She had to draw and erase and re-draw time and again until she was finally satisfied. Even as a beginner, though, her work showed great promise. "The class was very impressed," she recalled, "because the drawing did look so accurate. Not that I had any kind of facility. I just kept erasing and correcting until it was right. It's more that I knew what was wrong than that I could just sit down and very easily sketch it out. I still have to struggle. But I know when it's wrong and I can keep on working until it comes out right."

It is precisely this quality, I believe—this drive to do nothing less than one's best, in combination with the necessary talent (which Rowena modestly plays down)—that makes for greatness.

Originally, she had planned to become a musician. Since there were many musicians in her family, but not a single painter, it did not occur to her early in life that she might have any talent as an illustrator. Yet, as a child, she already had a keenly discerning eye for art. When she was six years old and living in Japan, the Christmas cards and many excellent animal drawings and portraits done by the family's three Japanese servants first awakened her sensitivity to, and love of, beauty. It took another twelve years (until she was a music major in college and one of her sorority sisters, an art major, was working on a painting) for her to realize: *Maybe I can do that, too.* However, four more years passed before she began to draw at an air force base hobby-shop class in California.

She says formal training was not beneficial in her development as an artist. Its chief value was that it exposed her to various materials and to the work of others. As a result of the discipline imposed upon her by regular assignments, Rowena learned the practice of drawing. After graduation, she spent the next four years teaching herself to paint.

Even as a virtual beginner, her professional talent was evidenced by the numerous portrait commissions she received during the four-year period of self-education. Her eventual progression to fantasy illustration was a natural process. Fantasy played an important part in her life throughout her childhood. She and her sisters were always telling each other fairy-tale stories that they made up. Then, as now, surrealistic and mythical paintings provided an intense fascination for her, and her early portrait commissions freely incorporated fantasy elements.

Since she has established herself not only as one of the top women fantasy illustrators, but one of the top fantasy illustrators *per se*, I was curious to know what her future goals were. "Basically, I would just like to keep on getting better," she said. "It's enormously important to me to make a beautiful painting, to create something now which may be known and understood and liked by people in the future. Of course, I would like to have more autonomy. I have a real desire to tell some stories and illustrate them—my own fantasies which, perhaps, might use existing mythology or fairy tales as a point of departure."

I find myself eagerly awaiting the fulfillment of this dream. As one who has spent more than half of my life as a professional illustrator, I am no longer easily impressed by the work of my colleagues. That special combination of imagination, artistic sensitivity, and highly developed skill connoting true excellence is all too rare. Rowena's paintings have all these qualities, which can be readily identified in this collection of her paintings, commissioned mostly as book covers over the past four years.

—Boris Vallejo
New York
1983

Foreword

"Jayne! *Jayne!* Come here—look. It's my book. It's my book!"

Thus the first real impact of Rowena Morrill on my personal universe. As a reviewer for a number of markets in and out of fantasy and science fiction, I'm subject to a constant flow of books, manuscripts, and galleys. What I had encountered on this particular noisy morning was a collection of color plates from Workman Press called *Tomorrow and Beyond* in which, in a full-page format, was the picture of a radiant little boy, so arresting, so beautifully modelled, with light and texture (texture of fabric, texture of flesh, texture of hair) that it took me more than a little while to take my attention away from that luminous young face and widen it to include the background. And here was a puppet with jewelled eyes, and there was the canvas of a carnival tent . . . "Jayne! That's my book!" and indeed it was. The very next day I received my author's copies of a new edition of *The Dreaming Jewels.* An author seldom has the privilege of an early look at a publisher's choice for a cover painting, and here was the compelling child, sure enough, gracing the front of my novel.

There were four more of her paintings in the Workman book, and I spent time with them, and then began to pay more attention to which artists did what on books and in the art exhibits I encountered at conventions.

I have to tell you that in the area of art, I come from ignorance and envy. I have always wanted to be a graphic artist, and my artist friends say to me, "Just go ahead—draw it the way you see it!" But these hands, so deftly obedient in fixing Volkswagens and *coq-au-vin,* just won't draw a good line even if you hold the ruler for them. They just won't do what I see with either outer or inner eye, and I give up in disgusted frustration. Therefore I stand awestruck before the likes of Rowena Morrill.

Rowena painted my portrait before we met. You'll find it on my collection *The Stars Are the Styx.* Since she worked from photographs, and all of them head shots, I found occasion to forgive her publicly for underestimating my muscles. That was at a convention, and she was "Art Guest of Honor"—rightly so. She had an hour for a presentation, and every would-be, could-be, and finished professional artist in the place filled the hall. She showed slides of her paintings, telling a little about each, frankly and clearly answering questions from the floor. There was—is—about her not a trace of the prima donna. She told us things about how she works—astonishing things. For example, after becoming familiar with the book (something all too few artists do, I'm afraid) and sketching out her composition, she begins to paint. She paints from the top of the canvas to the bottom, and then again from top to bottom . . . and then it's done. Finished with a finish it's hard to believe. And if she has to (she doesn't like to, but she will if she must), she'll do two of these a week.

When I first met her I had to look twice to see if it were really so: she's just as beautiful as those succulent maidens she paints. At the same time there is as little flirtatiousness about her as there is Big Ego. She is contained to such a degree that one must think of a word—not guardedness, it isn't that—*armored* is better. She speaks softly and gently, with complete and simple honesty.

In preparing these remarks I acquired a number of her slides and a projector and dragooned my friend, author, and accomplished painter Richard Englehart to fill in the wide-spectrum gaps in my understanding of art. One by one, as I screened the slides, he showed me some of the more evident skills in her composition—the continuing arc from tree-branch through dragon-wing to the angled sword of a fallen warrior; the basic triangle interlocking a circle buried in the chiaroscuro of forms and colors. And he marvelled with me at those things I had already noticed: her command of texture—flesh, fabric, wood, stone, steel—and light, often differently colored from different sources, with all the shadows from each exactly right.

For all her gentleness, she is very firm when firmness is called for. In a phone conversation (we live on opposite sides of the continent) she promised me some color negatives of my favorite paintings. Very excited, I blathered on in my lumpish fashion about a place I know where I could get enlargements which, at a short distance, look like original paintings, since they are done on a surface complete with brush marks.

There was an eloquent pause from her end of the telephone, and then she said gently, "Oh, please, no. There are never any brush marks."

Right, Rowena. No brush marks. Never.

Sincerely,
Theodore Sturgeon

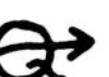

Description of Painting Technique

As a fantasy illustrator, I want my paintings to be as visually appealing and striking as possible. My technique must allow me to depict any subject matter in any lighting conditions in as few coats of paint as possible, applied as thinly as possible. After much experimentation I have developed a system that works well for me.

Since most of my paintings are illustrations for covers of books, I begin by reading a manuscript and taking note of interesting scenes and descriptions of pivotal characters. I choose the scene I like best and do a pencil sketch, very carefully working out the composition and the values—that is, where the lights and darks are. It is essential to cover the whole range of values in a painting, from deepest black to pure white, to create a sparkly, eye-catching effect. After I show my sketch to the art director and have it approved, I proceed to choose models and then go to my photographer's studio, where we spend an intense hour trying to simulate as closely as possible the conditions in the forthcoming painting. We make sure the lights are set up very carefully and try to get the costumes close to the final effect so I don't have to invent too much at the painting stage. Although it is impossible to get the costumes, hair, weapons, and other accoutrements precisely the same in the painting as in the photograph, the final result is much more believable and less cartoon-like if my reference is as clear and accurate as possible. My photographer is well equipped with many costumes, weapons, a wooden horse, and a good sense of humor. My models have to be able to move well and are also required to have a sense of humor and enjoy being wrapped up in furs in summertime and wearing bathing suits with a strong fan blowing on them in the middle of winter.

After I gather all the pictorial reference I need, I compose a very accurate, same-size line drawing of everything in the painting and transfer that to the gessoed surface I have prepared. Correcting the drawing errors at the painting stage is vastly inefficient, so I pay careful attention to what I am doing when I have the pencil in my hand. Because of the need to produce illustrations as quickly as possible, I usually use gessoed illustration board to paint on. I put four coats of acrylic gesso thinned with water on smooth illustration board and it is ready without having to be sanded. Masonite is the ideal surface for me to paint on, but it requires eight or ten coats of gesso and a lot of hard sanding to get it to the smoothness that I like.

Now that the line drawing is on the board, I put a wash all over the board of acrylic raw sienna and burnt sienna mixed with acrylic matte medium-thinned with water, resulting in a pale gold tone. This also fixes the pencil line drawing securely so that it will not be smeared by the underpainting. At this point, after all the laborious preparations, I am eager to start the painting.

The first day of painting is the most fun because I get to cover the whole board with paint and see how my idea is going to work. I love oil paints and use them for all my paintings. The colors are mouthwateringly beautiful and they go on like butter, taking most of the labor out of rounding the form, unlike the attractively quick-drying acrylic paint that requires ten thousand tedious crosshatches to get a gradation in color. Using turpentine thinned with a few drops of linseed oil as a medium, I begin by rendering all the forms in a monochromatic, burnt umber underpainting. This allows me to deal separately with the color and value problems in a painting. Burnt umber is ideally suited for this stage because it can go from darkest dark to the palest of thinned-out washes; it dries faster than any other color; and it gives the whole underpainting a warm, pleasing effect. I have seen people do underpaintings in strange, ghostly colors that would demoralize me so much I would have a hard time tackling the painting the next day. I am much more comfortable if the painting doesn't go through any awkward stages along the way.

When the underpainting is thoroughly dry, I start the next day's work painting in the background, using all its proper colors with the intention of finishing it completely at that stage. I lay in the darkest colors first, then put in the medium tones and finish with the highlights. Then I paint the figures, usually taking one day per figure. After all that is dry it is time to administer the subtle variations that make a painting unique. I apply transparent glazes of color and translucent washes—that is, colors mixed with white. For me, doing those final touches is the most exciting part of the painting. If all has gone well before and I am not too desperately rushed for time, it is a delight to see how far I can push the paint and make it sparkle.

For most of the painting I use a limited palette of colors chosen for their intensity and quick drying time. They are: titanium white, cadmium yellow pale, cadmium orange, cadmium scarlet, cadmium red, alizarine crimson, cadmium green pale, Windsor emerald, Windsor blue, burnt umber, and Mars black. For the finishing touches I use every luscious color I can get my hands on, provided it is permanent. I apply the paint at every stage with the finest sable brushes, flats for large areas and rounds for smaller areas and details. I keep my brushes very clean and throw them away as soon as the tips are worn off before they start getting scratchy. After a painting is dry I apply a coat of spray damar varnish and cross my fingers and hope my newest creation will surpass the preceding ones.

After I gather all the pictorial reference I need, I compose a very accurate, same-size line drawing of everything in the painting and transfer that to the gessoed surface I have prepared.

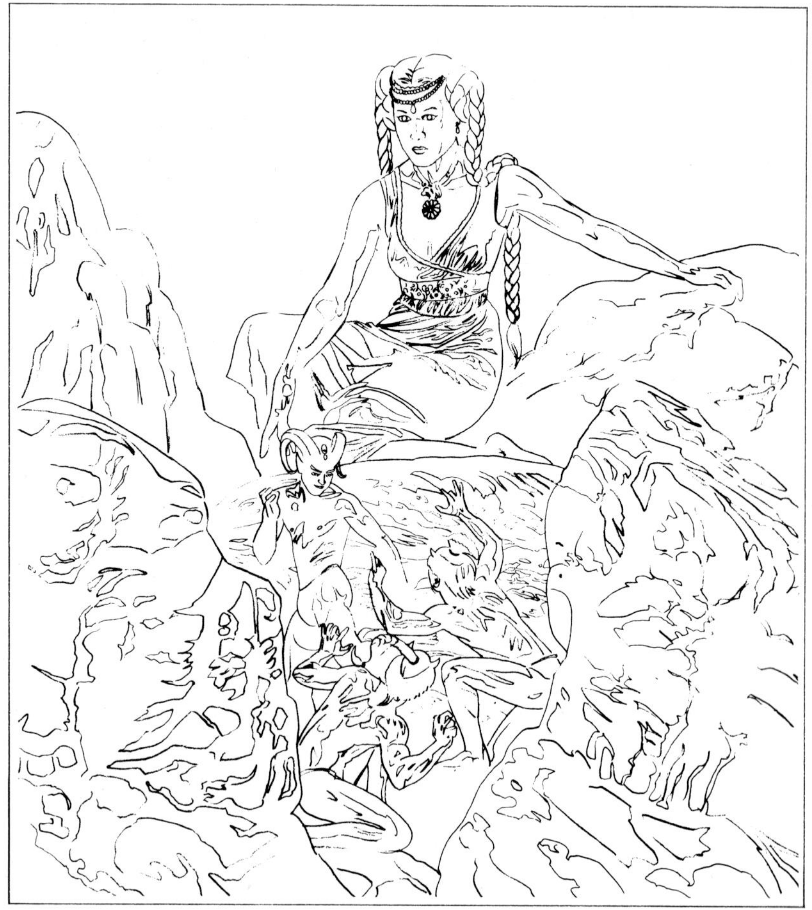

Now that the line drawing is on the board, I put a wash all over the board of acrylic raw sienna and burnt sienna mixed with acrylic matte medium-thinned with water, resulting in a pale gold tone.

The first day of painting is the most fun because I get to cover the whole board with paint and see how my idea is going to work. I love oil paints and use them for all my paintings.

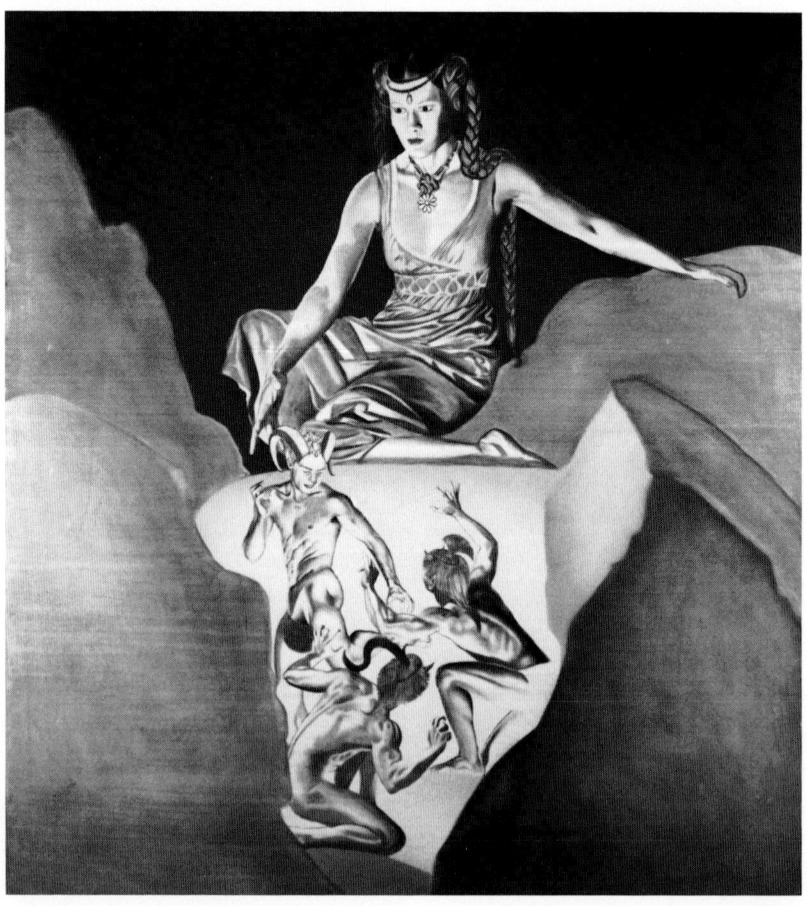

When the underpainting is thoroughly dry, I start the next day's work painting in the background, using all its proper colors with the intention of finishing it completely at that stage.

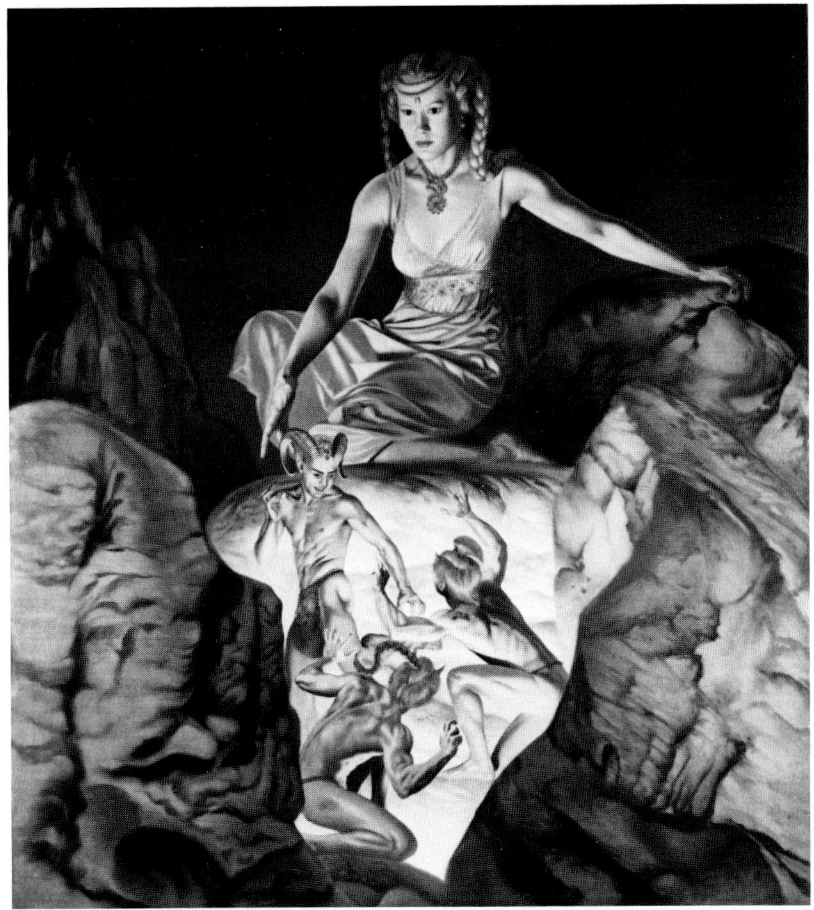

After all that is dry it is time to administer the subtle variations that make a painting unique. I apply transparent glazes of color and translucent washes—that is, colors mixed with white.

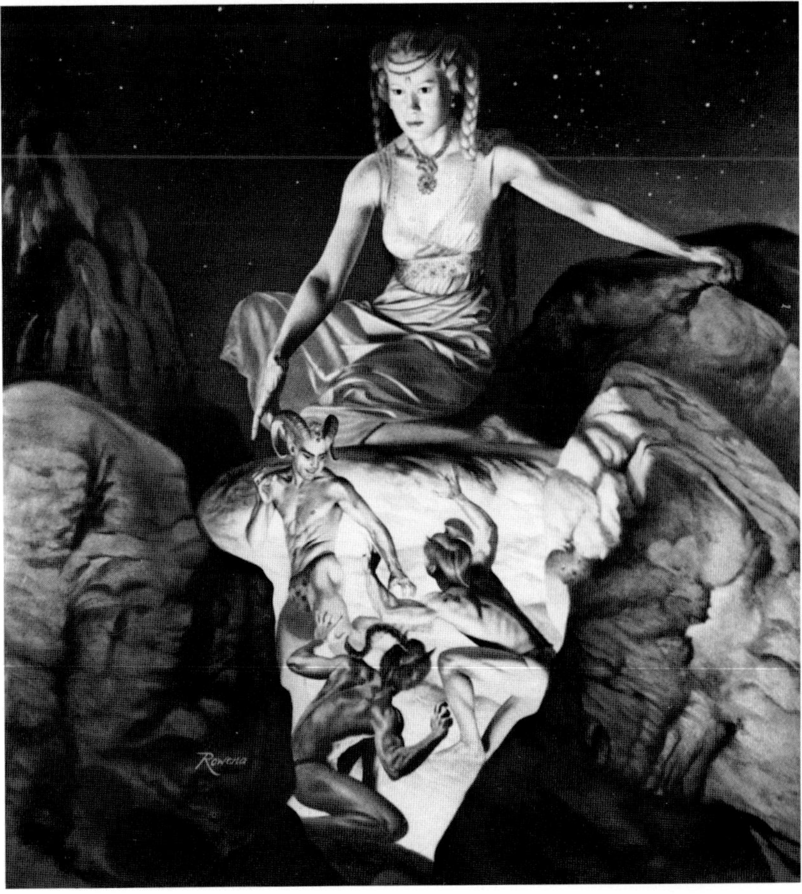

THE IMPS FROM UNDER THE ROCKS

The girl in the painting has been wandering around the rocks at night searching for the glow that gives away the entrance to the subterranean habitat of the magical imps. She was looking particularly for the well-built variety that lift weights, and she is now conjuring them up to do her bidding. In a loose way, this is analogous to how I feel when I go through the thinking processes necessary to get an idea for a fantasy painting.

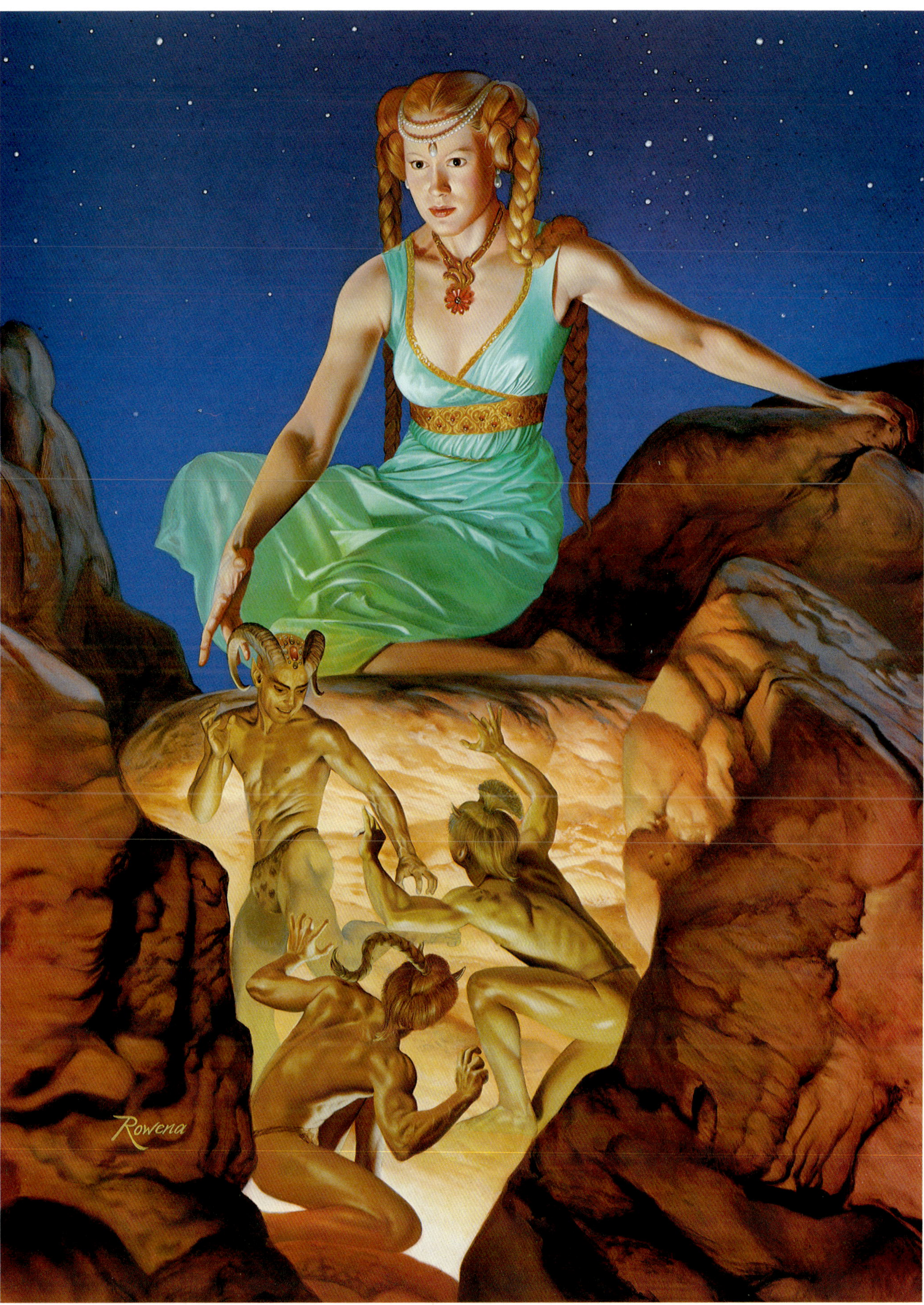
Rowena

THE CITY OF THE SINGING FLAME

When I designed the creature in this painting,
I was referring to human and animal anatomy
and tried to make it look
as if this monster really existed.

(Timescape)

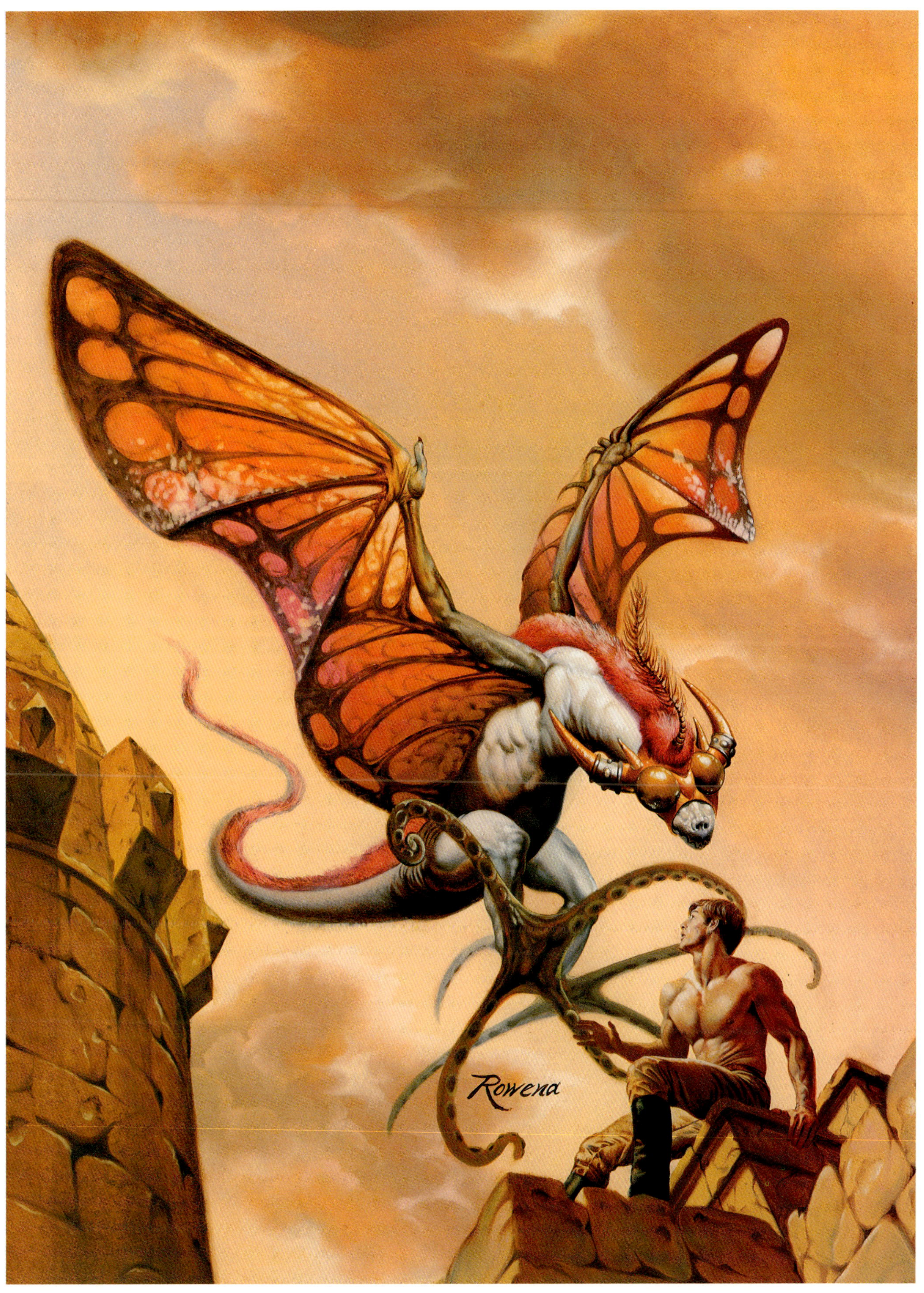
Rowena

MADWAND

This is by far the most serious girl-and-monster painting I have ever done,
and also the first nude.
I suppose I was influenced by the macabre tone of the book.
This gets away from my "all in good fun" approach
and, since I was not very comfortable with the result,
I was surprised to find that so many people like this painting.

(Phantasia Press)

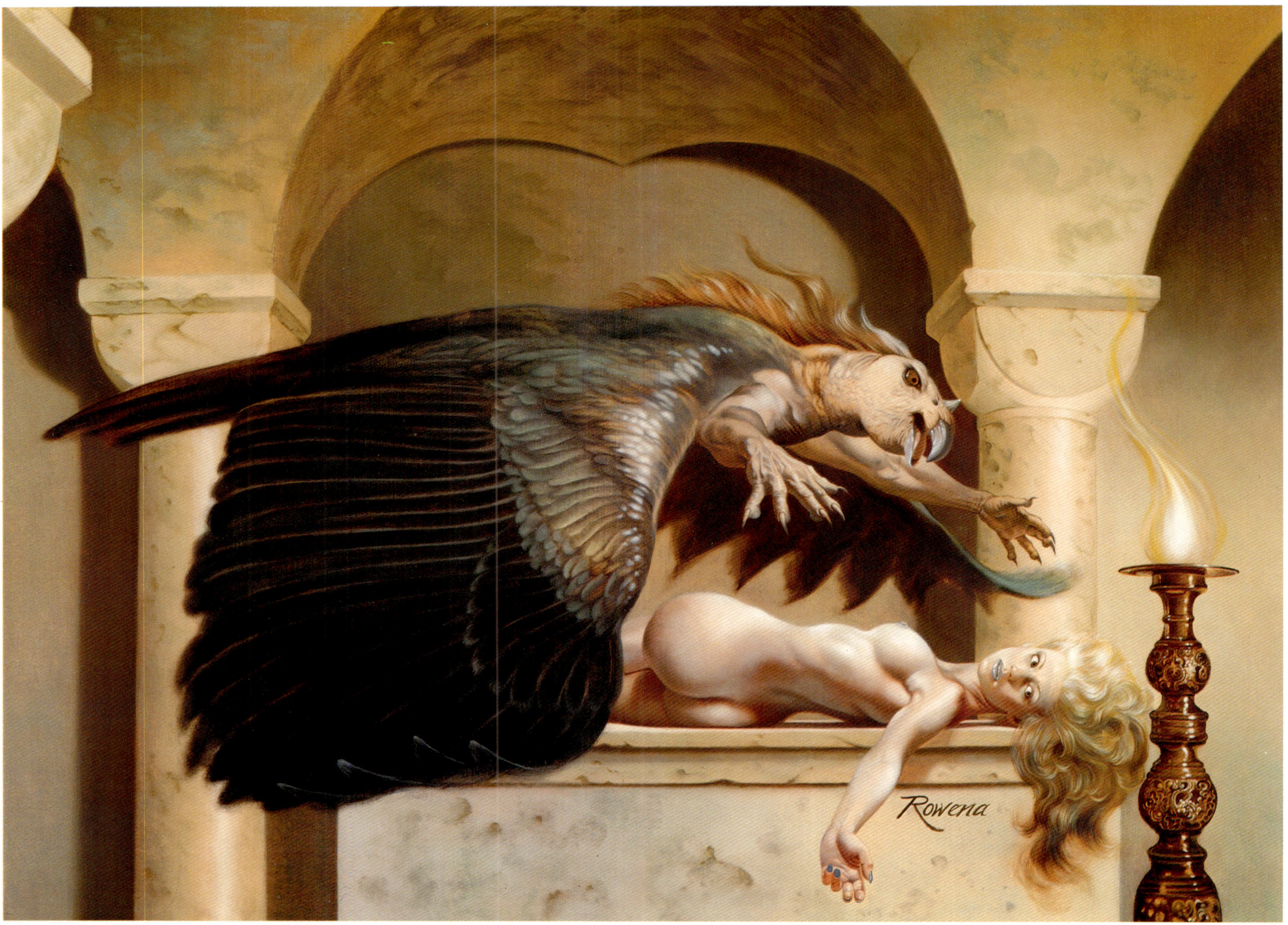
Rowena

GHOSTS I HAVE BEEN

*Although this is the type of sentimental cliché I do not fancy,
I must admit I enjoyed painting it despite my initial reluctance.
To get the color and lighting effects just right,
I had to run back and forth from my studio to a dark room
with a candle in it, hold my hand in the proper position,
and then try to remember what it looked like.
It was fun putting in the smoke using a lot of linseed oil
and a big, fluffy brush to blend it.*

(Dell)

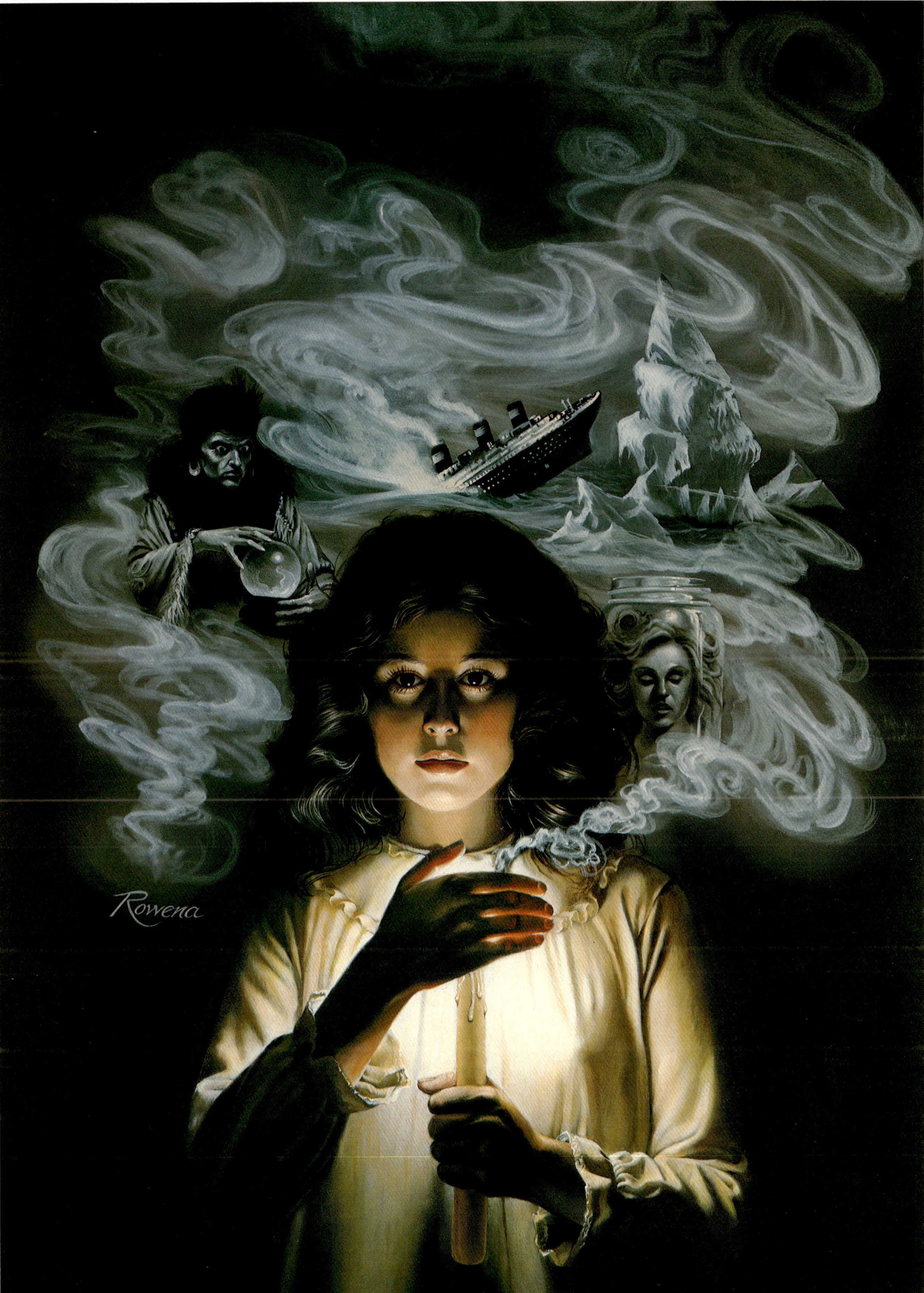
Rowena

RETIEF OF THE CDT

Here I must rave on about how beautiful the male figure is
and what a joy it is to paint.
It goes without saying that I mean the male figure at its best,
namely lean and muscular.
There are so many beautiful curves, furrows, and round, interlocking shapes
where the deltoids go between the biceps and triceps
or where the serratus muscles lock into the ribs.
As if the basic large shapes weren't interesting enough,
there are also all those veins and sinews so apparent in the arms and legs,
hands and feet. Additionally, since there is not a layer of fat
covering the whole structure, there is a lot of interesting color
showing through from beneath the skin.
The model I used for Retief was a great inspiration,
and I enjoyed doing this painting immensely.

(Timescape)

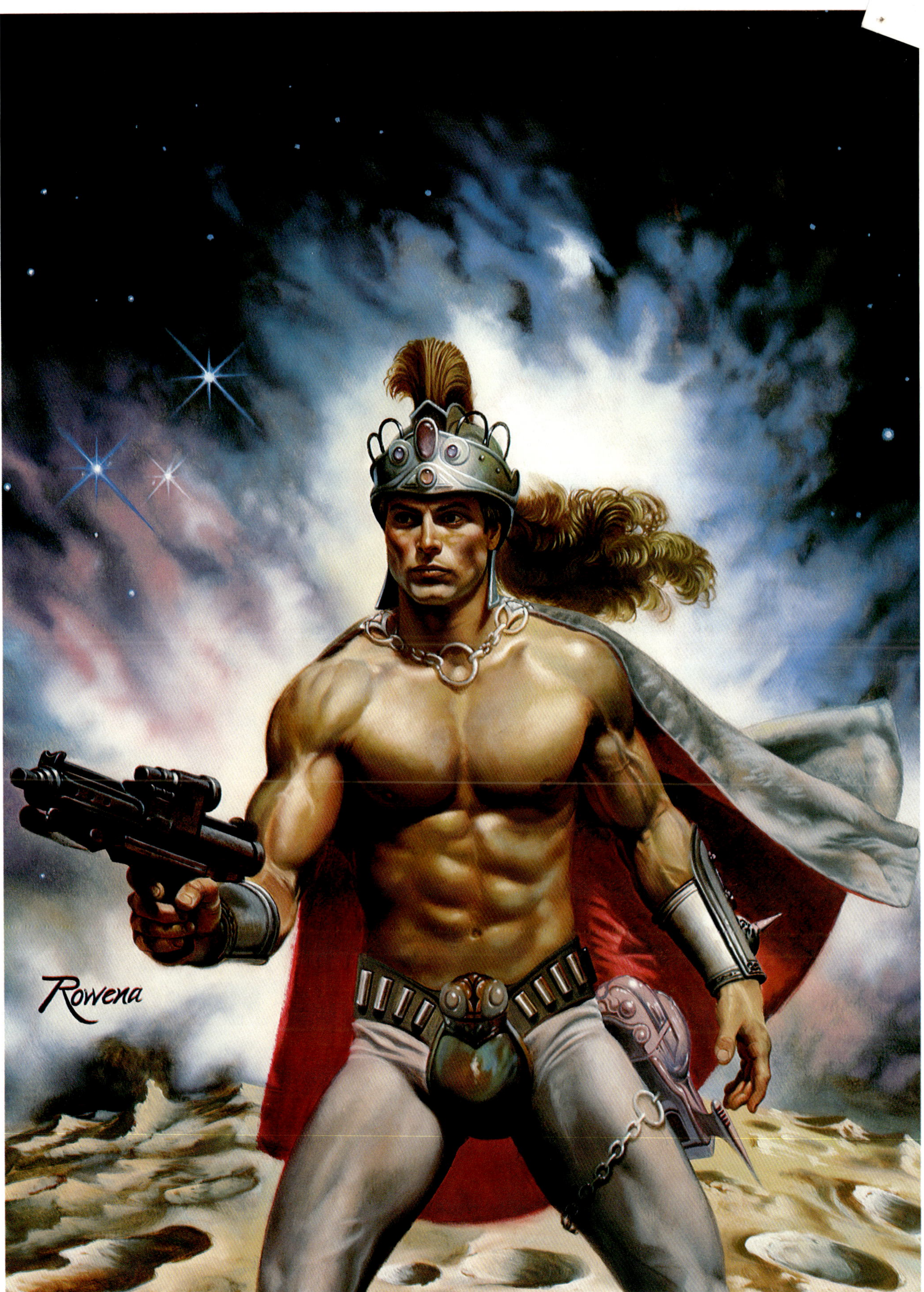
Rowena

YEARWOOD

Yearwood *comes close to the degree of contrast and color that I try to achieve in my paintings. It ranges from the darkest dark in the background to the purest white around the girl's feet, and the color is vivid and varied. My inspiration for the girl was an illustration in one of my favorite books of fairy tales that I read as a child. My version of the idea, a bewitching girl with light coming out of the ground at her feet, is so different from the source of inspiration that it would be hard to see the relationship. But I derived the greatest pleasure from making one of my beloved images from childhood come to life in my own way.*

(Timescape)

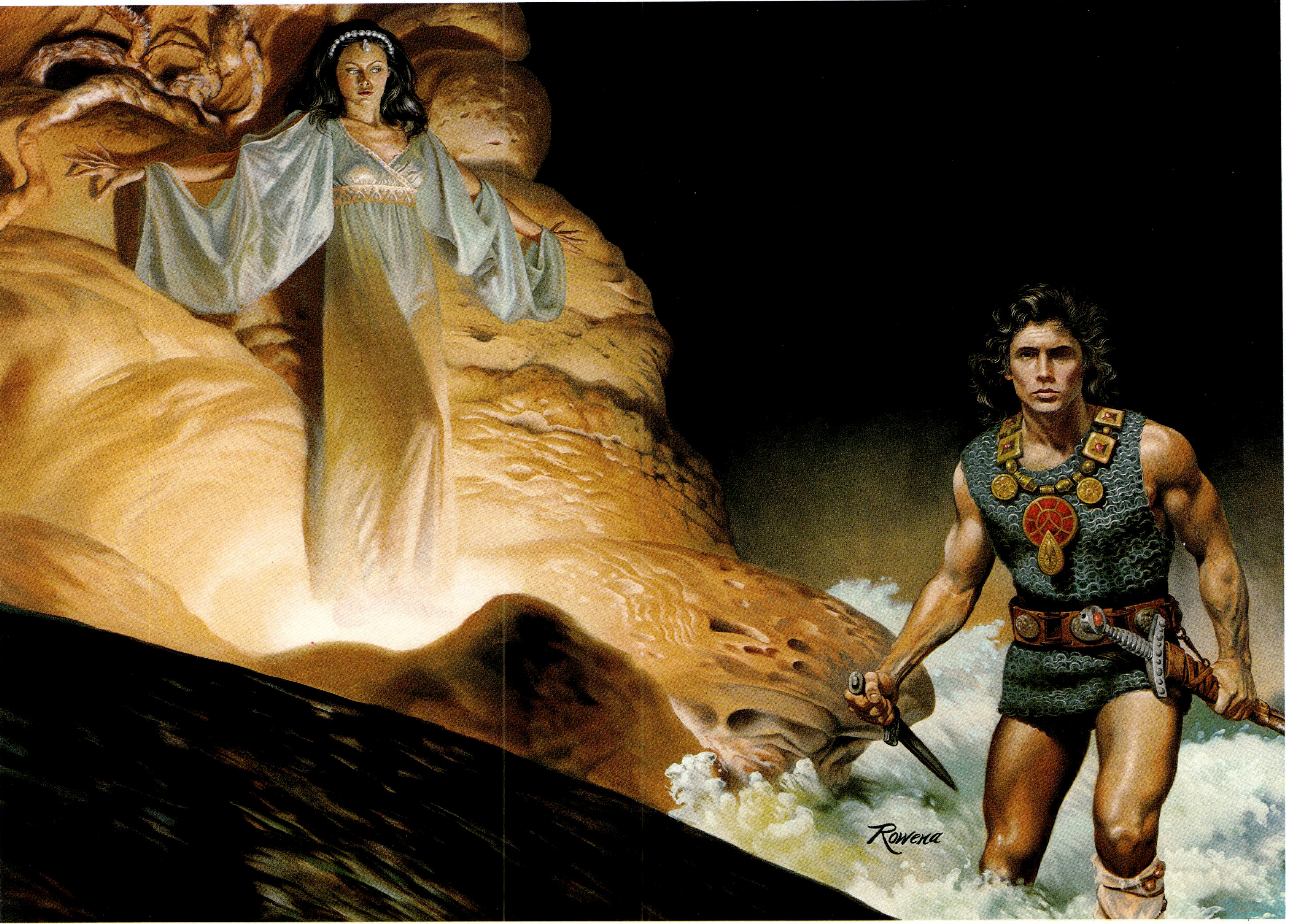
Rowena

KING DRAGON

This painting drew a lot of criticism from feminist groups,
a fact which leaves me surprised and bemused.
As I do with all of my threatening-monster paintings, I did it with a light,
satirical touch, not to be taken seriously.
If I place myself in the position of the girl on the rock, I think of the creature
as a beautiful specimen coming to keep me company, entertain me,
or rescue me. To me a creature represents something challenging
and frightening in the beginning,
a fascinating source of energy and excitement
to be mastered and enjoyed.

(Berkley Publishing Group)

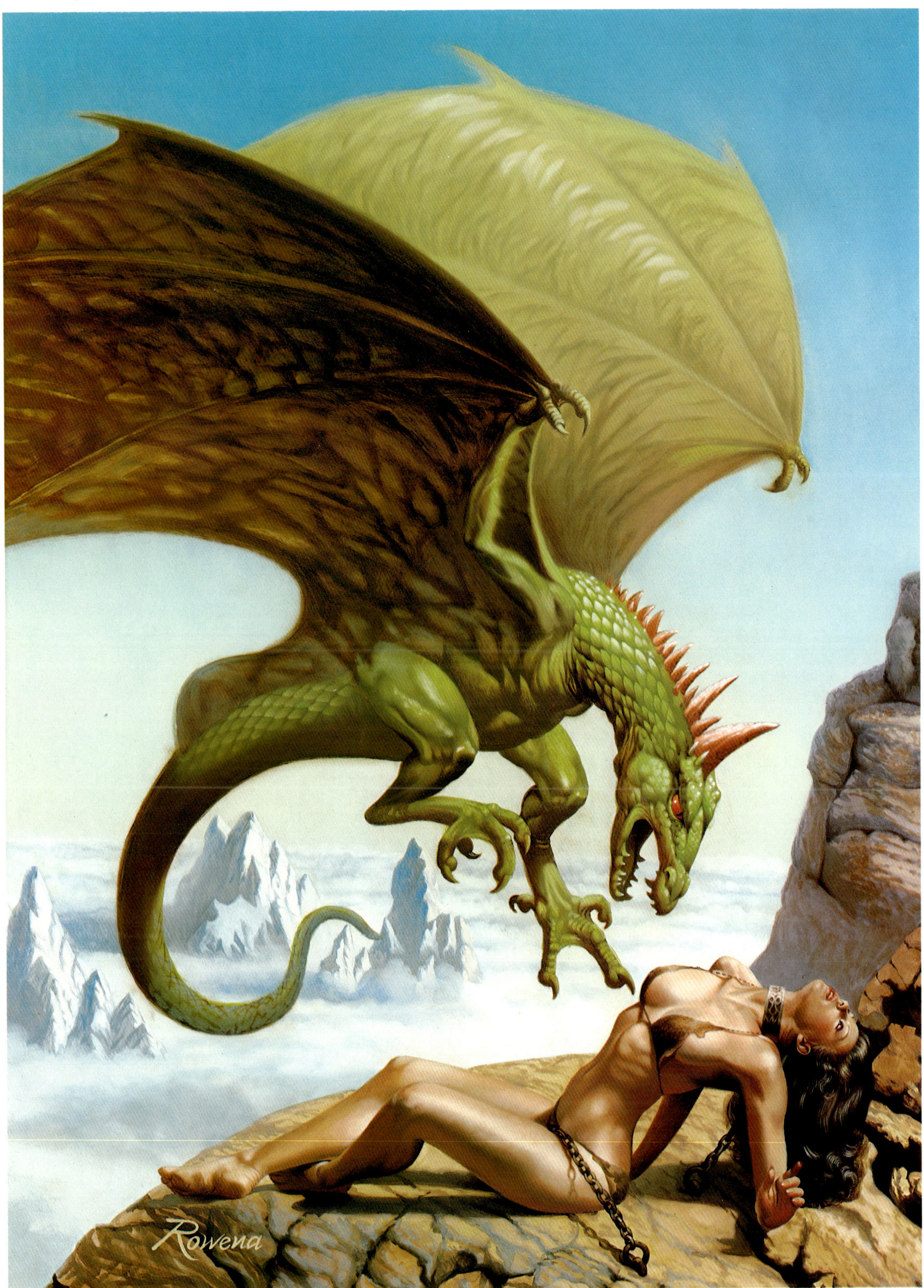
Rowena

PROJECT POPE

Although this was strictly an editorial idea
and nothing similar to anything I would devise for myself,
I thoroughly enjoyed painting the bishop's satin robe.
I think the painting turned out to be colorful and appealing.

(Ballantine)

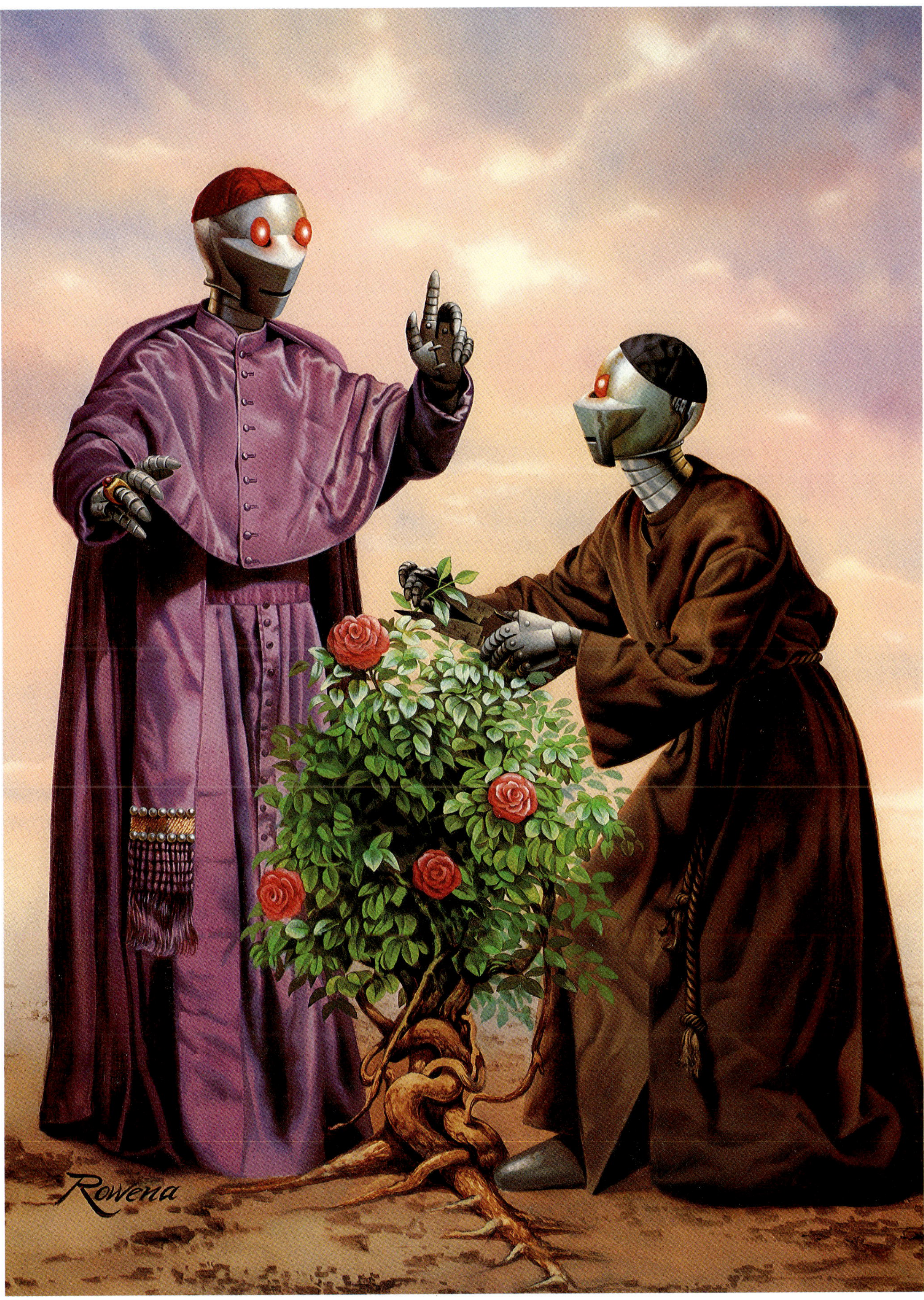
Rowena

GOLEM 100

My one and only black figure so far
required a whole new combination of tints and colors
to produce what I felt to be a believable dark figure.
I found it easier to arrive at the shimmering, glossy effect
that to me signifies living flesh
using a darker range of colors.

(Pocket Books)

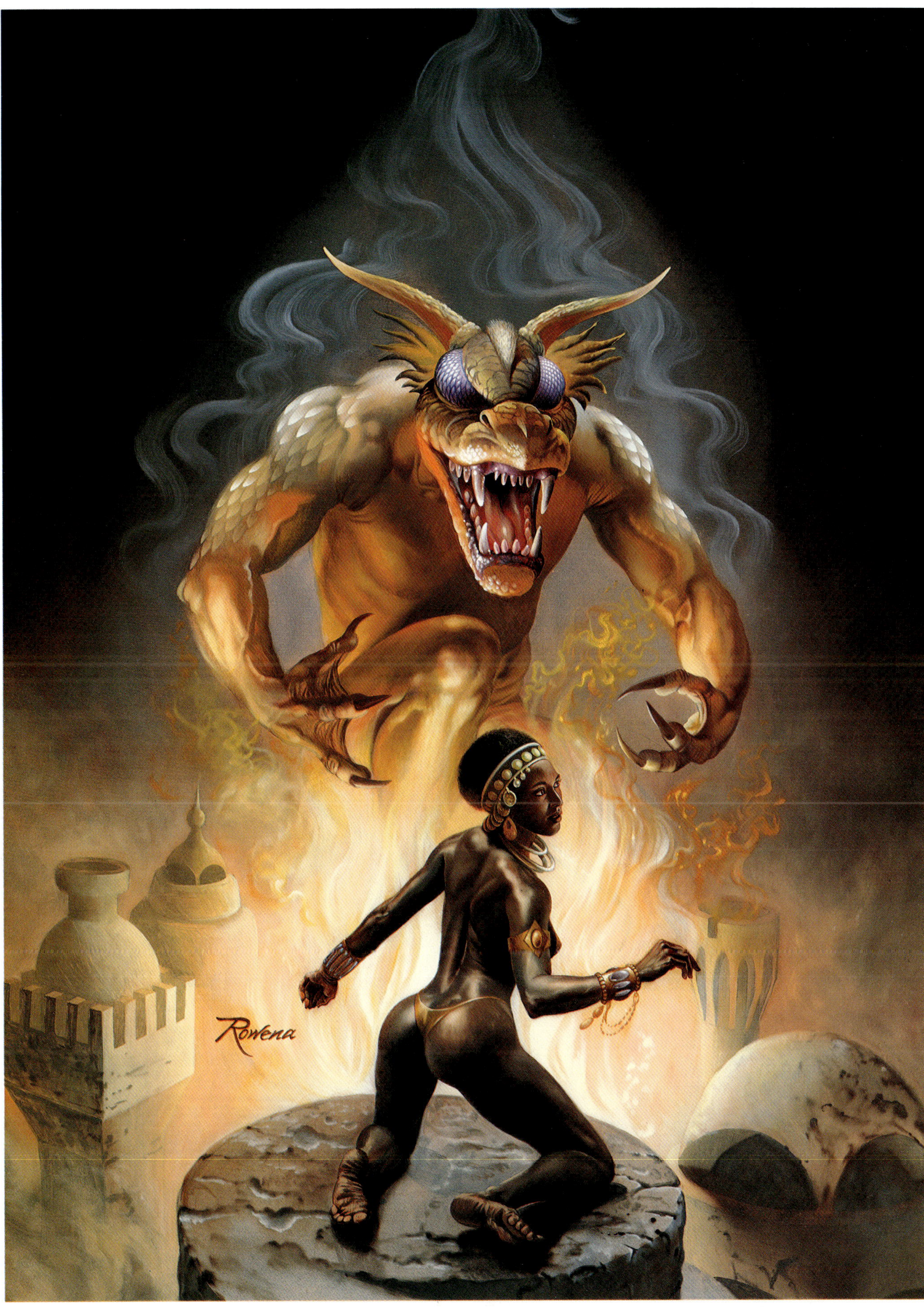
Rowena

THE DREAMING JEWELS

Painting children is not one of my favorite occupations, but this little boy had such an engaging personality that it was a pleasure to use him as a model. I have always loved Holbein's portraits and was thinking of them when I painted the boy. I think that the wary, innocent child juxtaposed against the bizarre carnival imagery made an interesting combination.

(Dell)

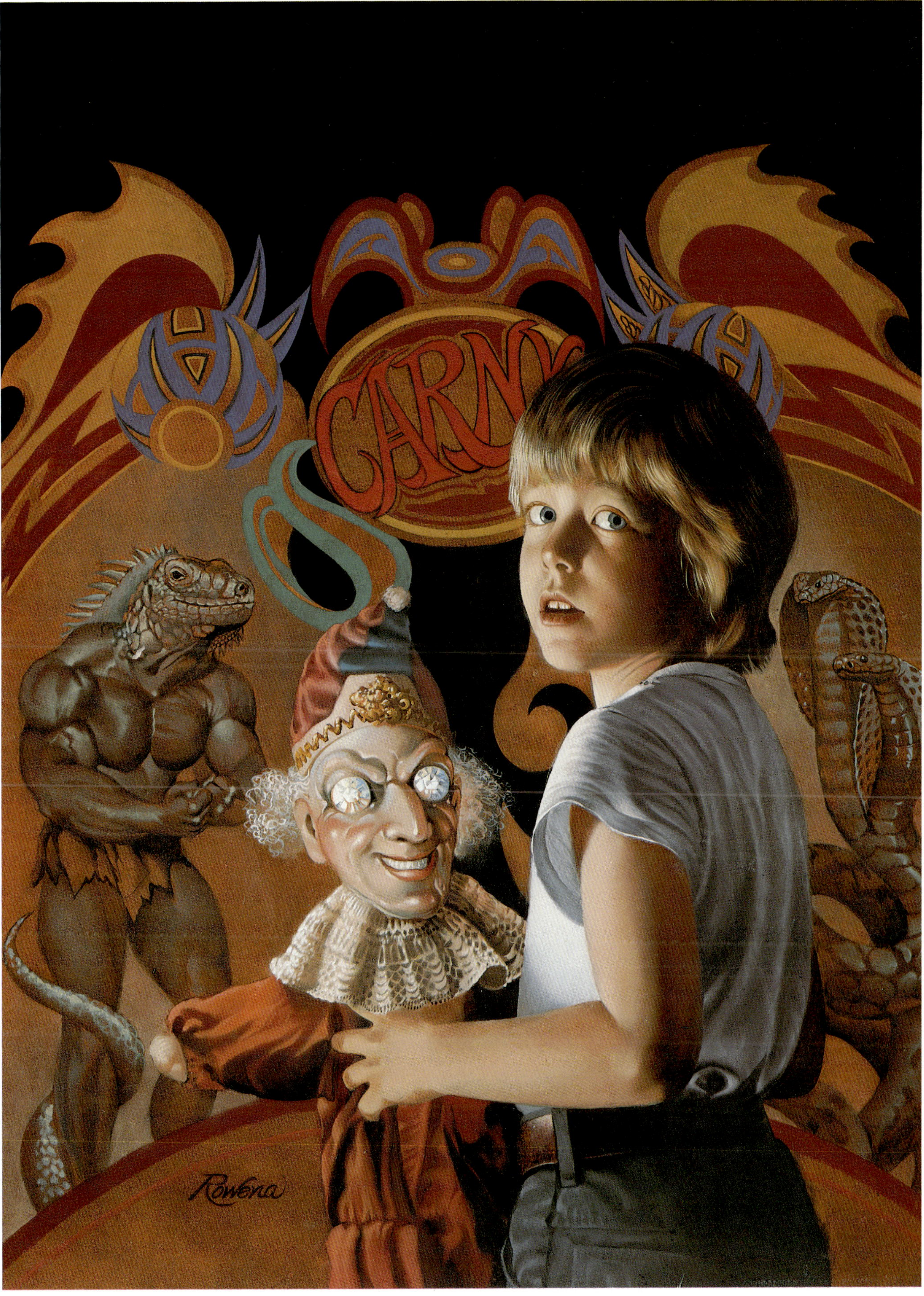

CARN
Rowena

THE TIME BENDER

*I used my favorite model for both the man with the axe and the giant.
Because of the infinite variations of light
hitting the endless diversity of human form,
I find it necessary to have models for all the figures I paint
to get a credible result. However, I frequently
make drastic changes from the original reference.*

(Berkley Publishing Group)

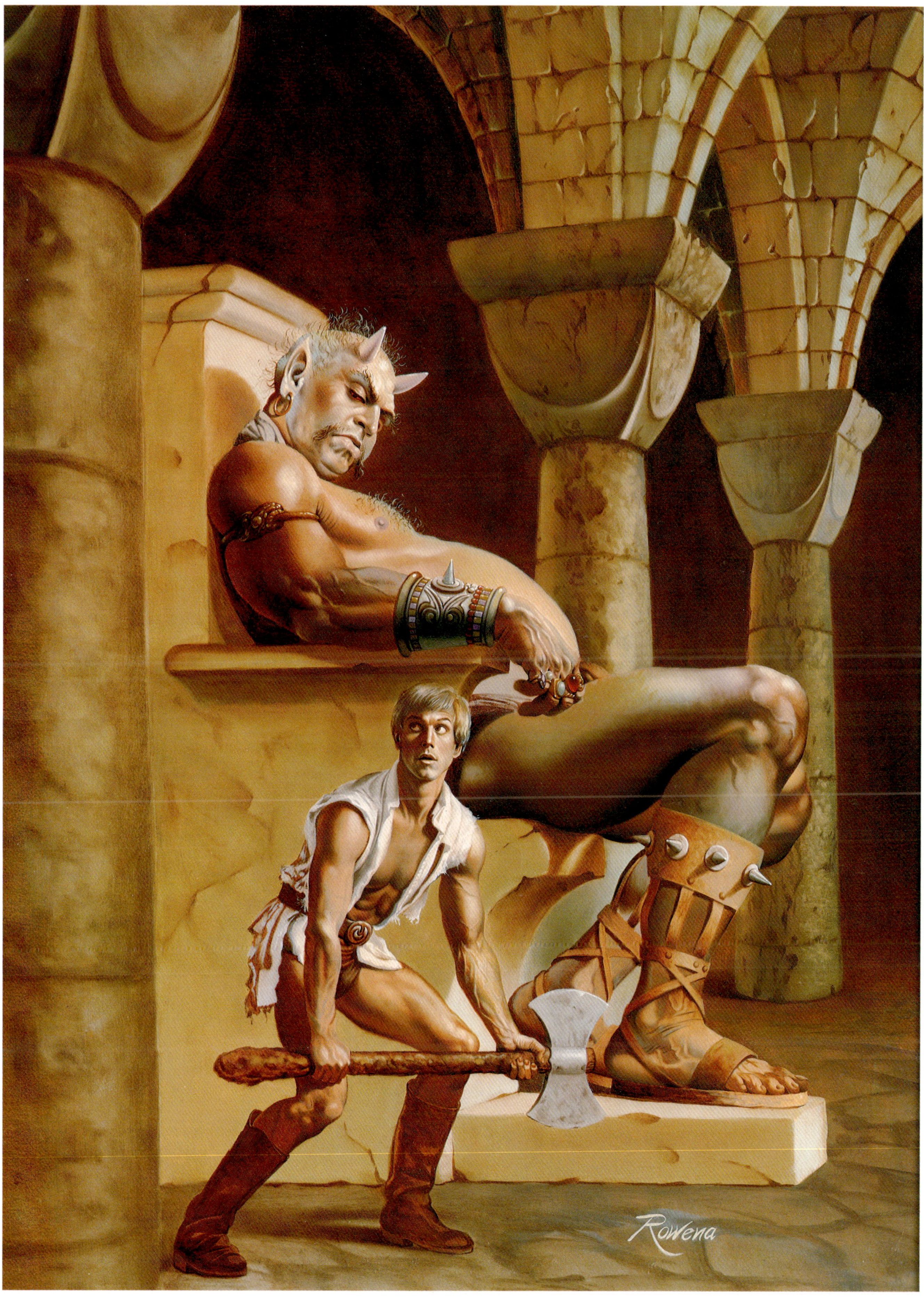
Rowena

THE CRIMSON CHALICE

*The best part of doing this painting was depicting
the kind of silky white palfrey
that I would like to be riding through the woods if I were Guinevere.
That is also the type of castle I would like to have surrounded
by that particular forest. It is gratifying to paint a setting
that I would like to be in myself, and dreaming about it
helps to while away the long hours it takes
to paint such a complicated picture.*

(Berkley Publishing Group)

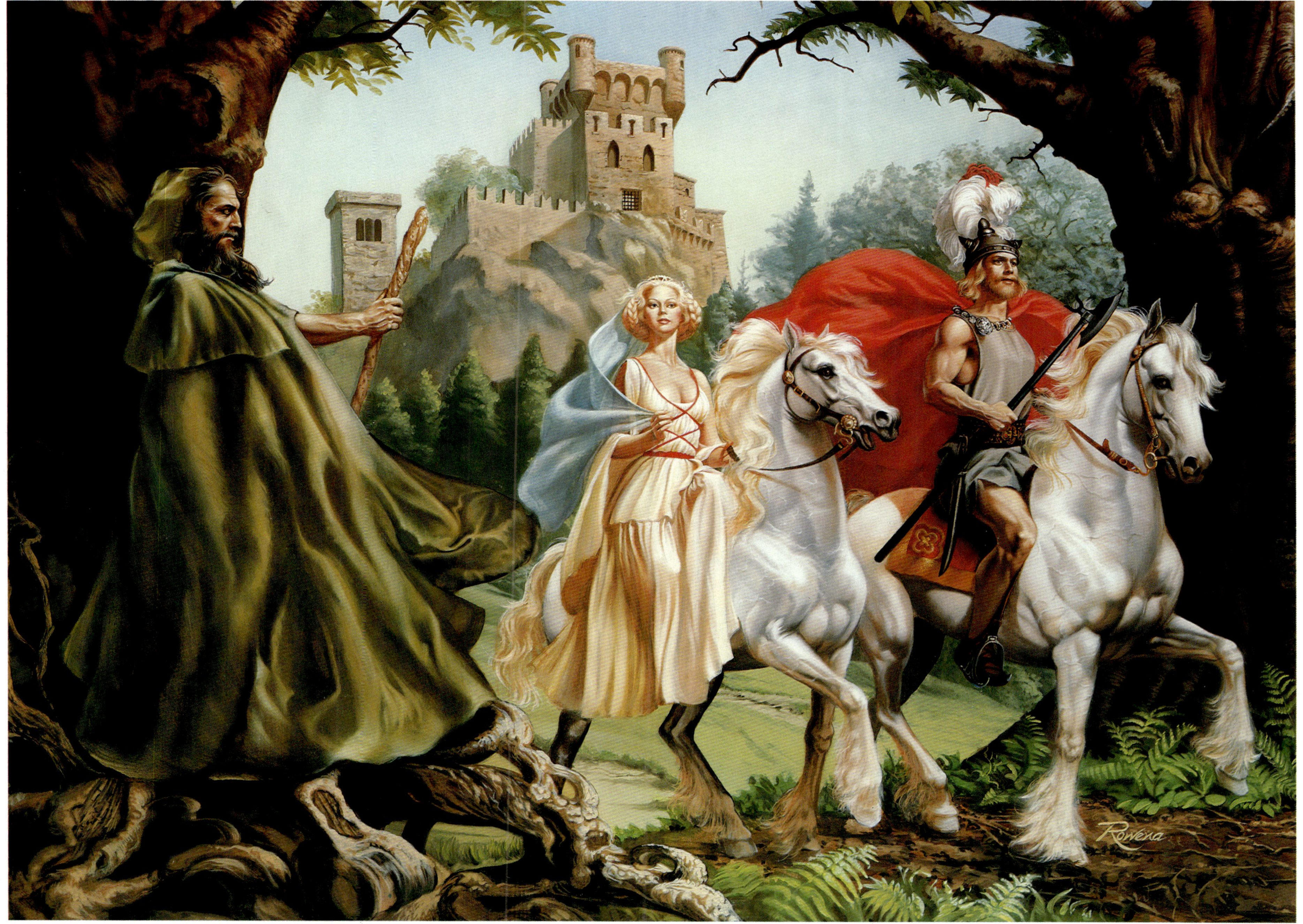
Rowena

GOD OF TAROT

I have always loved Chinese dragons and modeled this one after a picture on my Chinese teapot. To me he is so gorgeous that my only regret is I did not give him hind legs.

(Berkley Publishing Group)

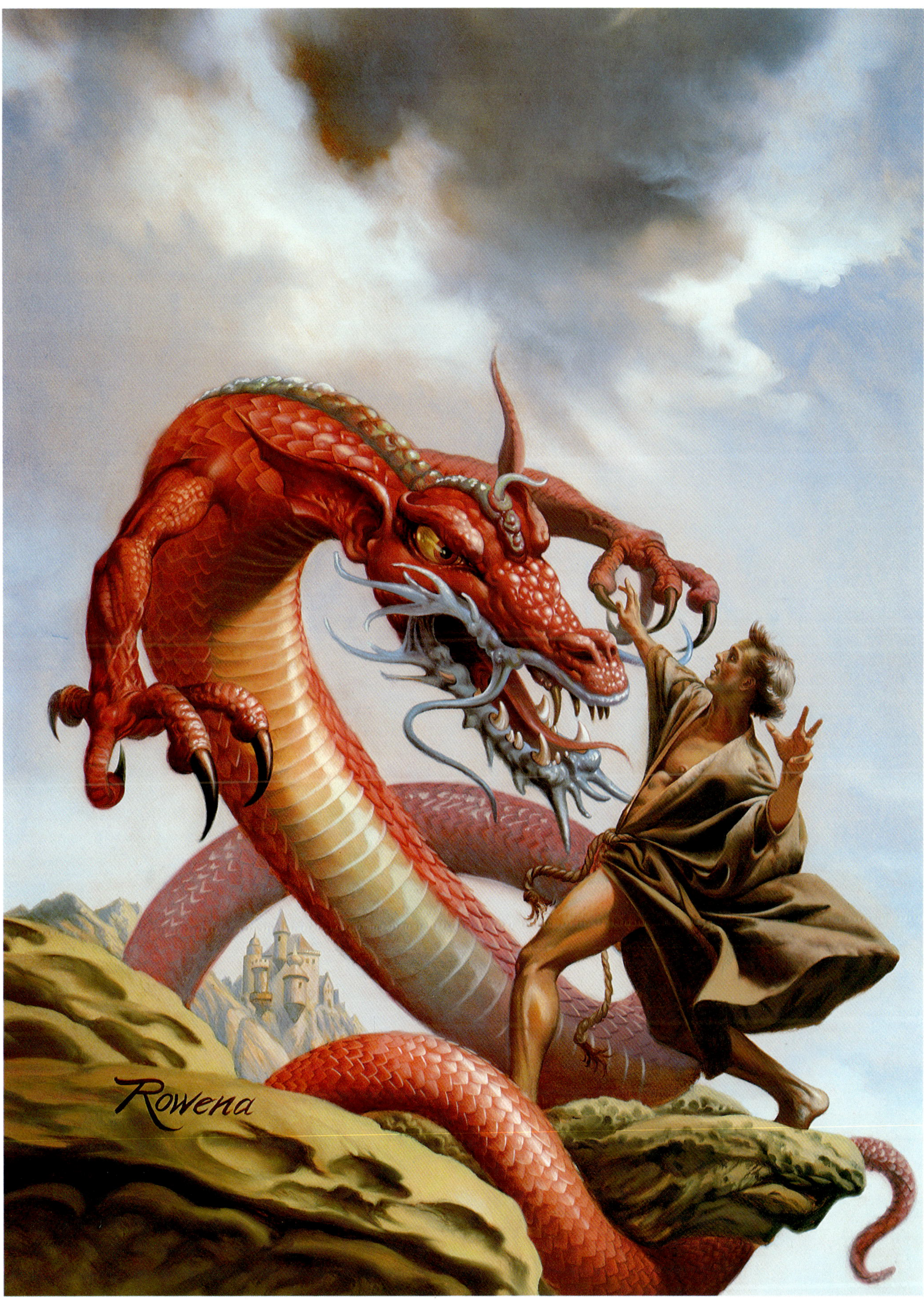
Rowena

ALCHEMY AND ACADEME

My model for the wizard is a professional actor
who delivered such a hilarious monologue on magical spells
while posing for the photograph that I could hardly
stop laughing long enough to take a few pictures.
I loved painting his expressive face,
putting as many colors into his white beard as I possibly could
while still keeping it white.

(Ballantine)

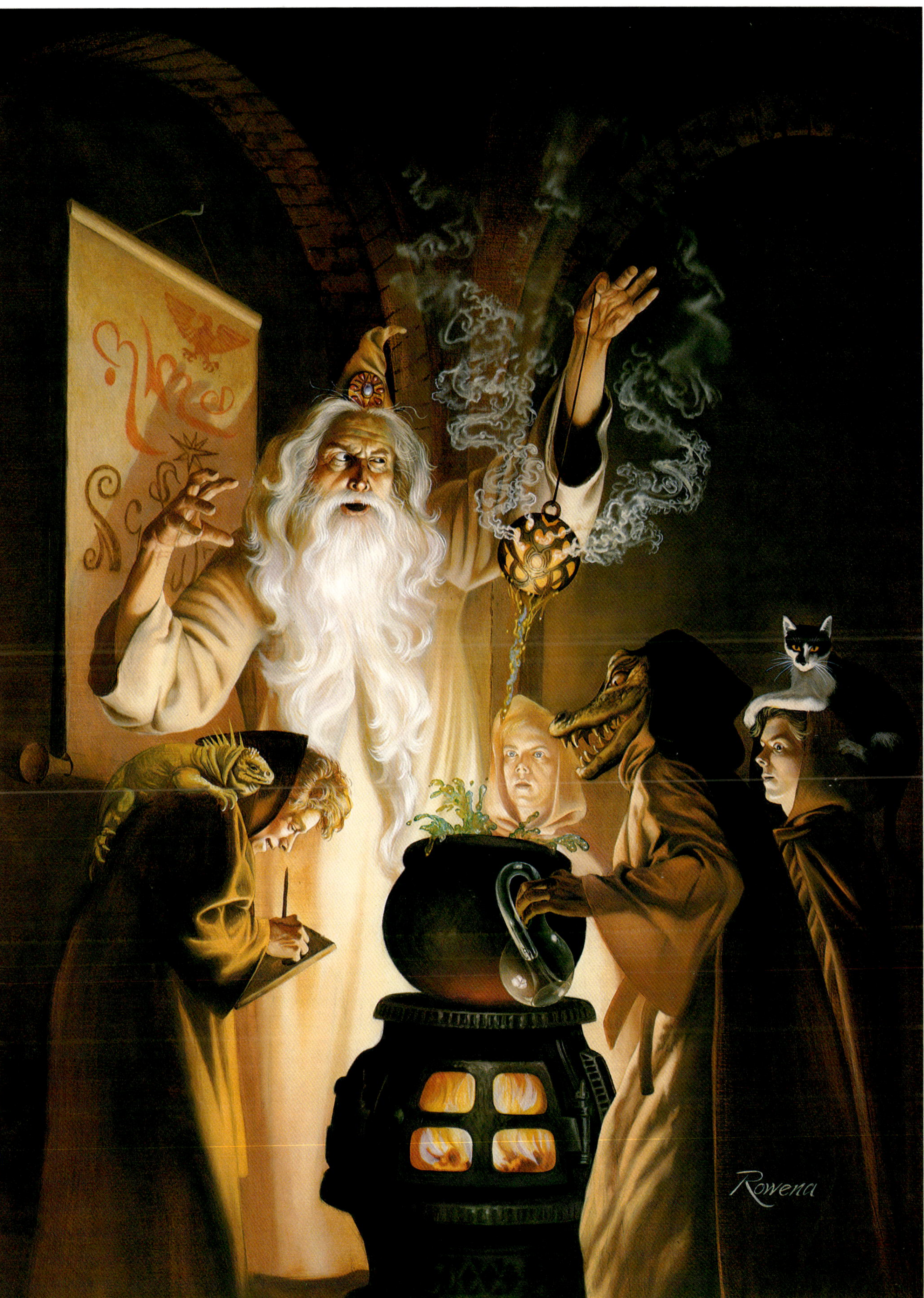
Rowena

THE GOLDEN SWAN

When I first started doing illustrations I looked at comic books frequently for inspiration in doing the male figure, using a lot of standard exaggerations and distortions. As time goes by, I stay increasingly close to reality while still making some subtle changes that lead to my ideal of the figure. This painting is one of my most recent male figures and comes very close to what I think a man should look like, minus the long hair.

(Timescape)

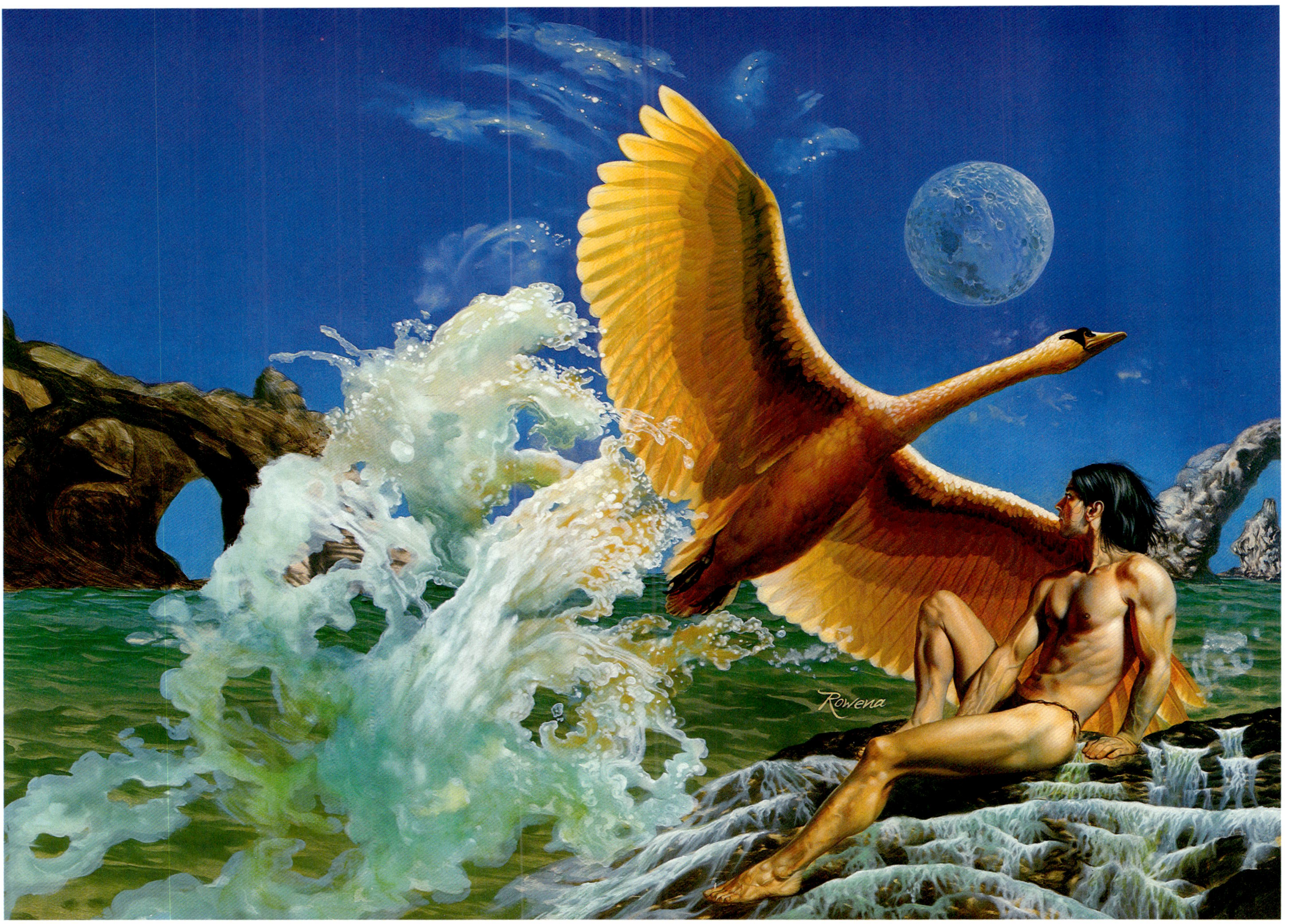
Rowena

THE UNKNOWN FIVE

One of the most potent combinations of images I know of is that of a woman and a monster. The requirement for this painting was to depict a woman and a monster in the style of the early pulp covers. I took a satirical approach and tried to create a truly outrageous monster. Having been interested in the round, writhing forms in early Indian sculpture, I used that as my prototype for the girl.

(Dell)

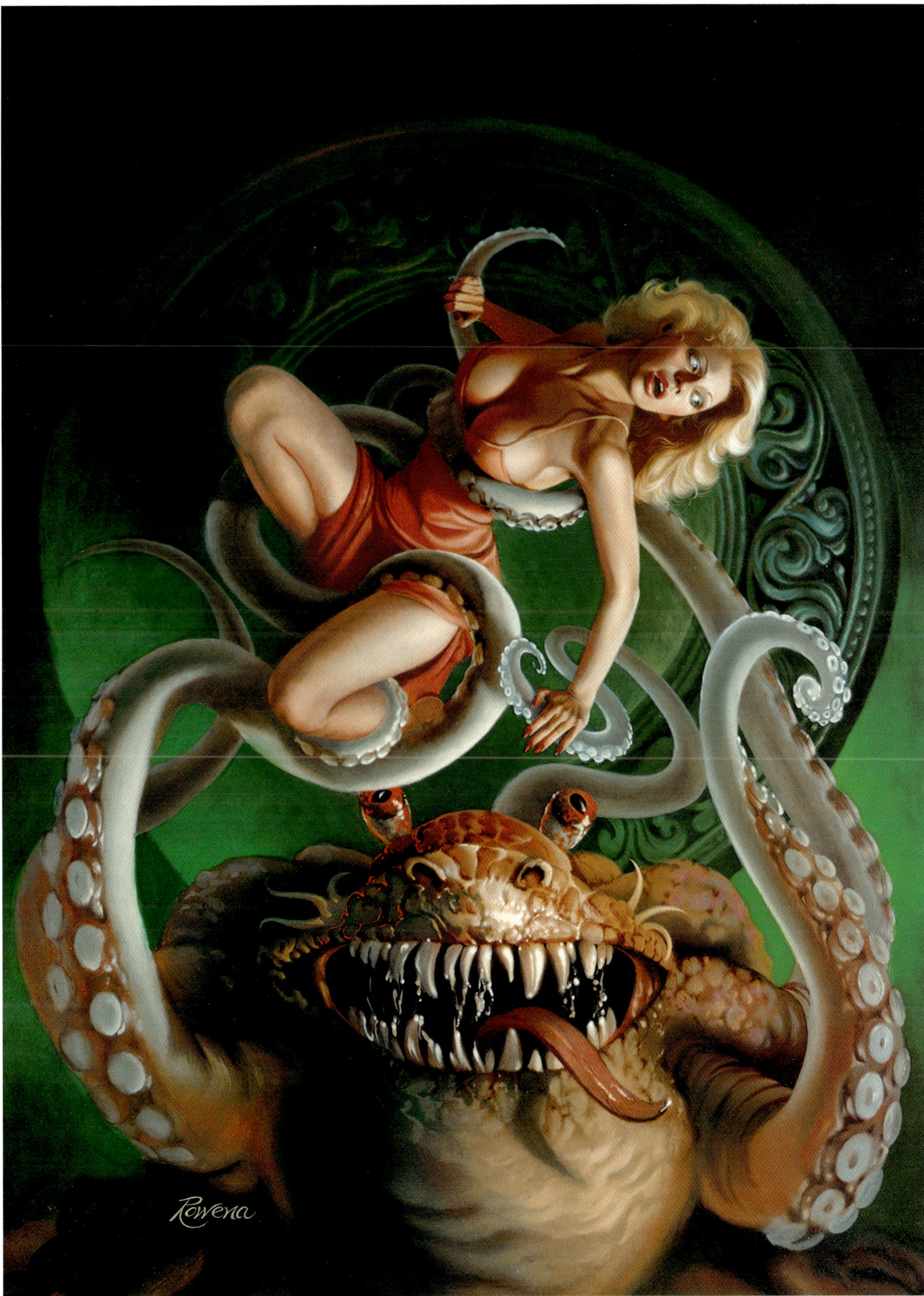
Rowena

THE EYES OF SARSIS

The devices used to depict action in a painting are flying hair and clothing, blurred edges, and twisting poses. Here, I wanted to portray a lithe warrior woman in motion contrasted with a stiffly mechanical soldier who had suddenly gone into a trance-like state and was coming to get her.

(Pocket Books)

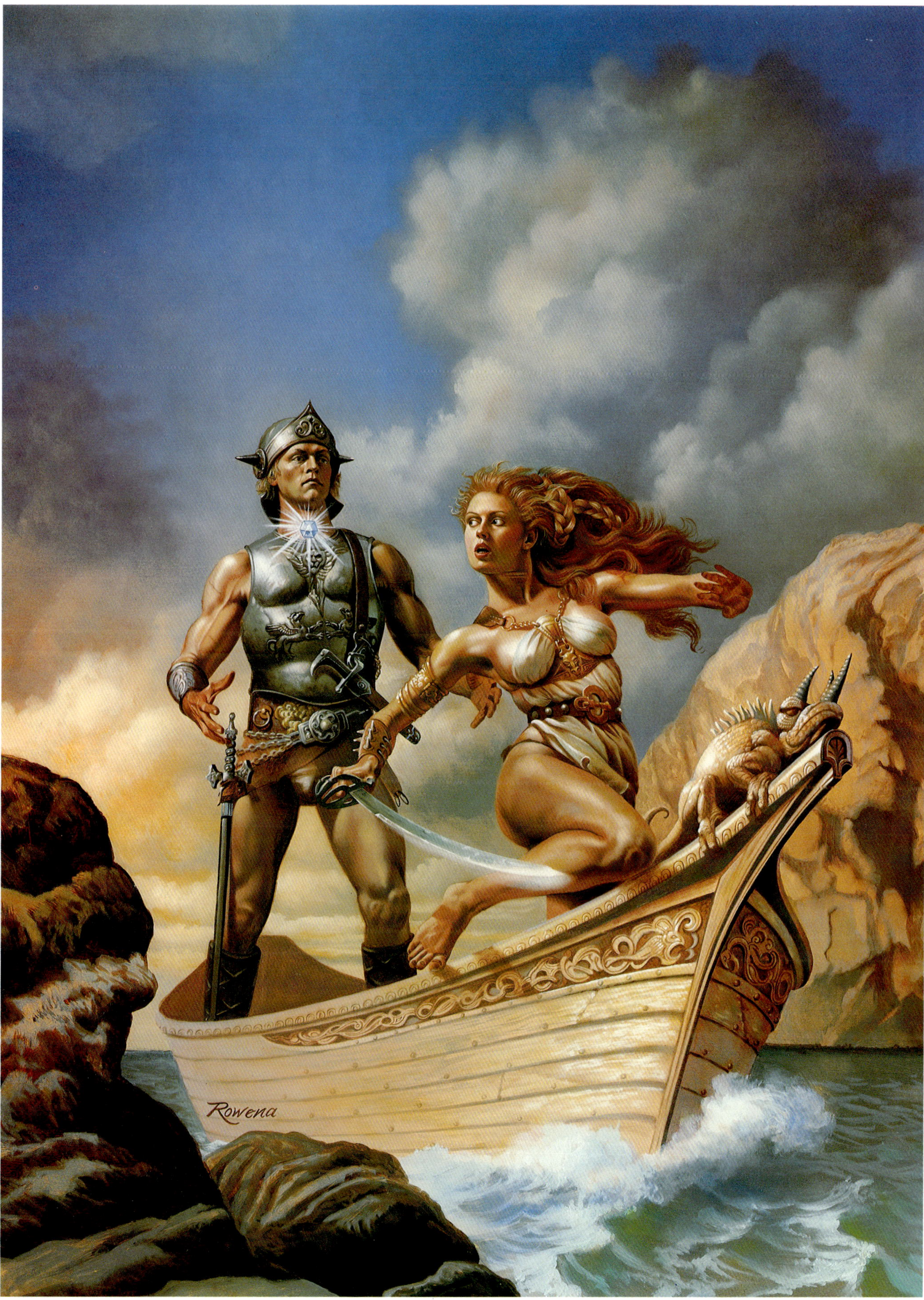
Rowena

TWILIGHT TERRORS

One of my favorite themes, if I can treat it humorously, is that of people's fears when they are alone in the dark. My type of monster is a grinning, gleeful one, not the kind that is truly horrifying and looks as though it would smell awful. I looked at pictures of sea creatures and reptiles for reference and put together a combination of textures, colors, and shapes that I personally find as appealing as—and perhaps even more interesting than—my human subjects.

(National Lampoon)

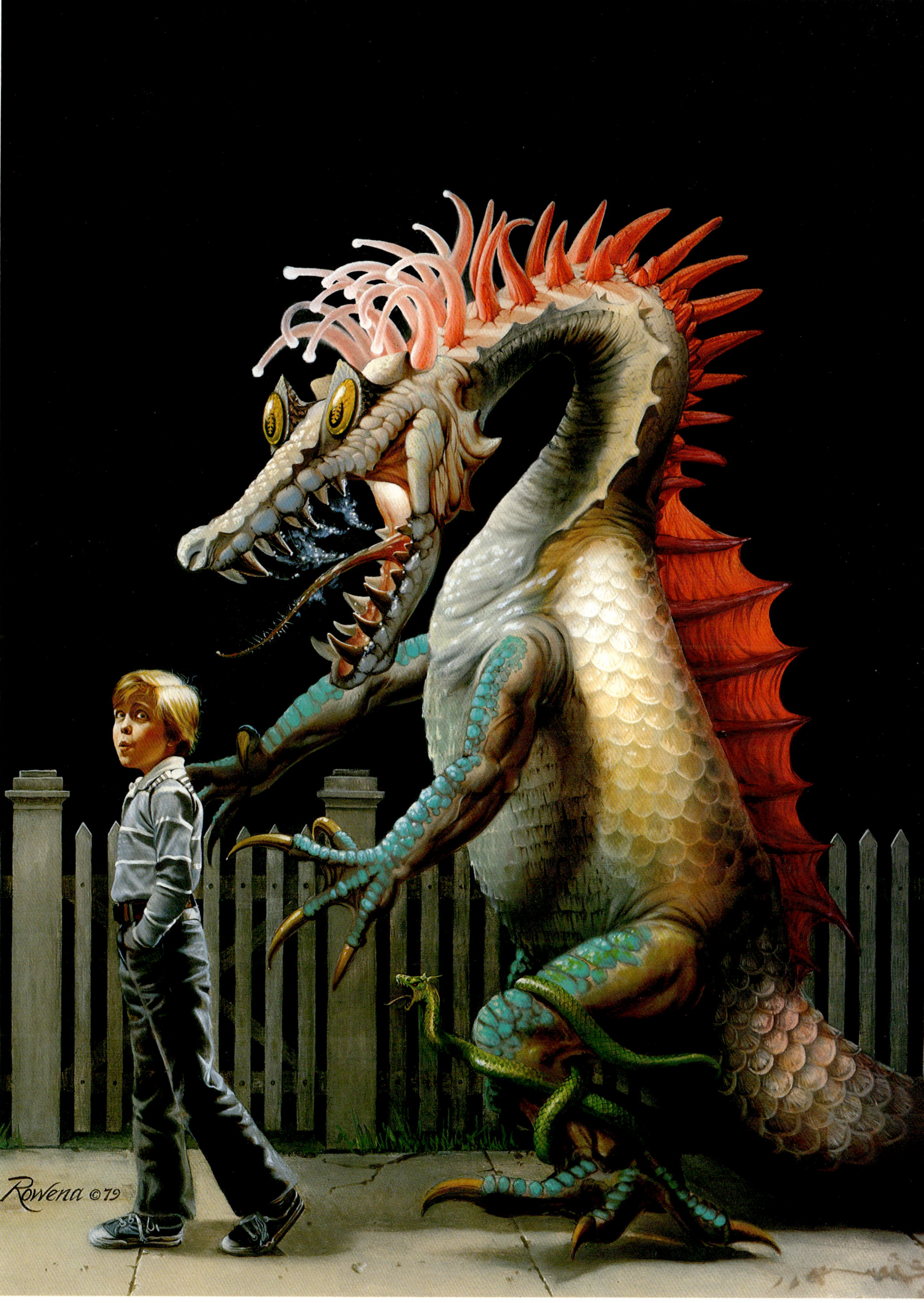
Rowena ©79

BLUE ADEPT

I used the same model for the warrior and for the genie.
With a face like his, you can see why I had to pose him
with his back to the viewer. The woman model was sick that day;
this turned out to be a real bonus
because it gave her the slightly demented look
I wanted her to have in the painting.

(Del Ray)

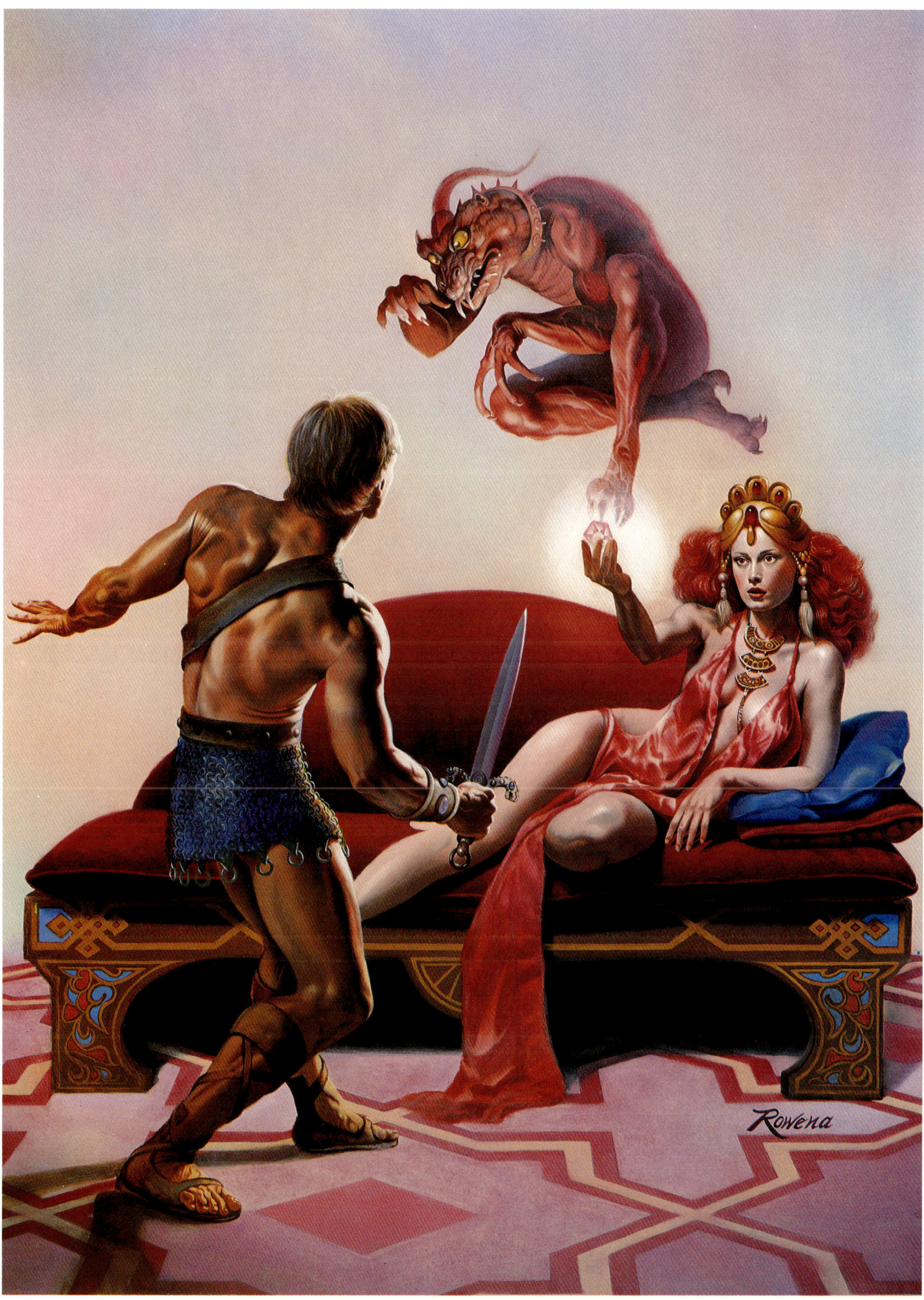
Rowena

WHO FEARS THE DEVIL

This fellow is out in the woods by himself at night,
and he thought he heard something.
If he had any idea what it really was, wouldn't he be surprised . . . !
An interesting technical problem in this painting
is that the purest white paint is inexpressibly darker than a fire.
It is necessary to make all sorts of compromises
to derive an effect remotely close to reality.

(Dell)

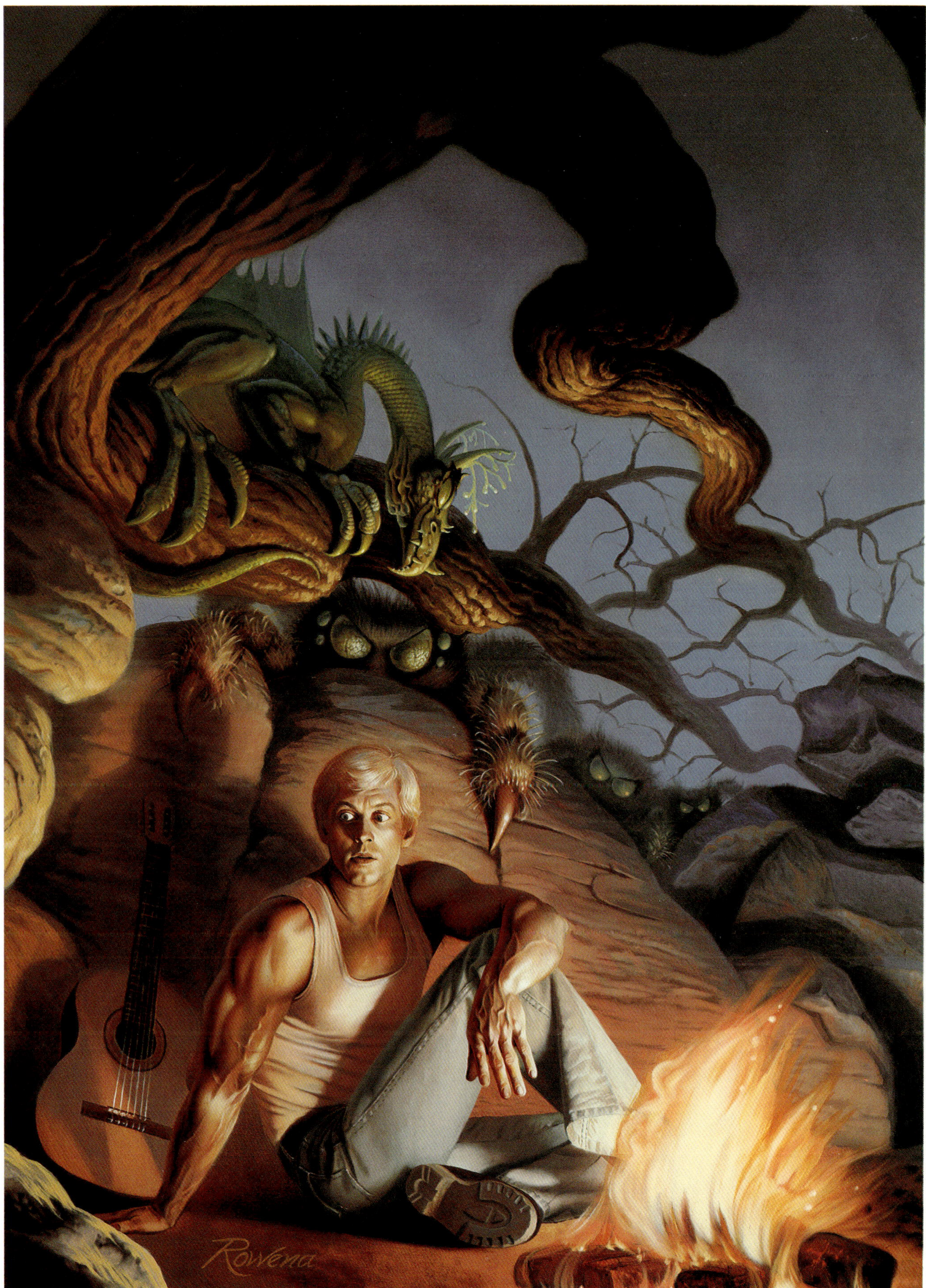
Rowena

MASTER OF THE FIVE MAGICS

When reading the Arabian Nights
I was always fascinated by the theme of a sorcerer conjuring up a genie.
I was thrilled to have the opportunity to do the subject in a painting.
The background and the genie had to be completely finished and dry
before I could put in the dark smoke,
an omission that made the painting look strange until the very end.
In order to have the genie look large and imposing,
I drew him all hunched up near the top of the ceiling.

(Del Ray)

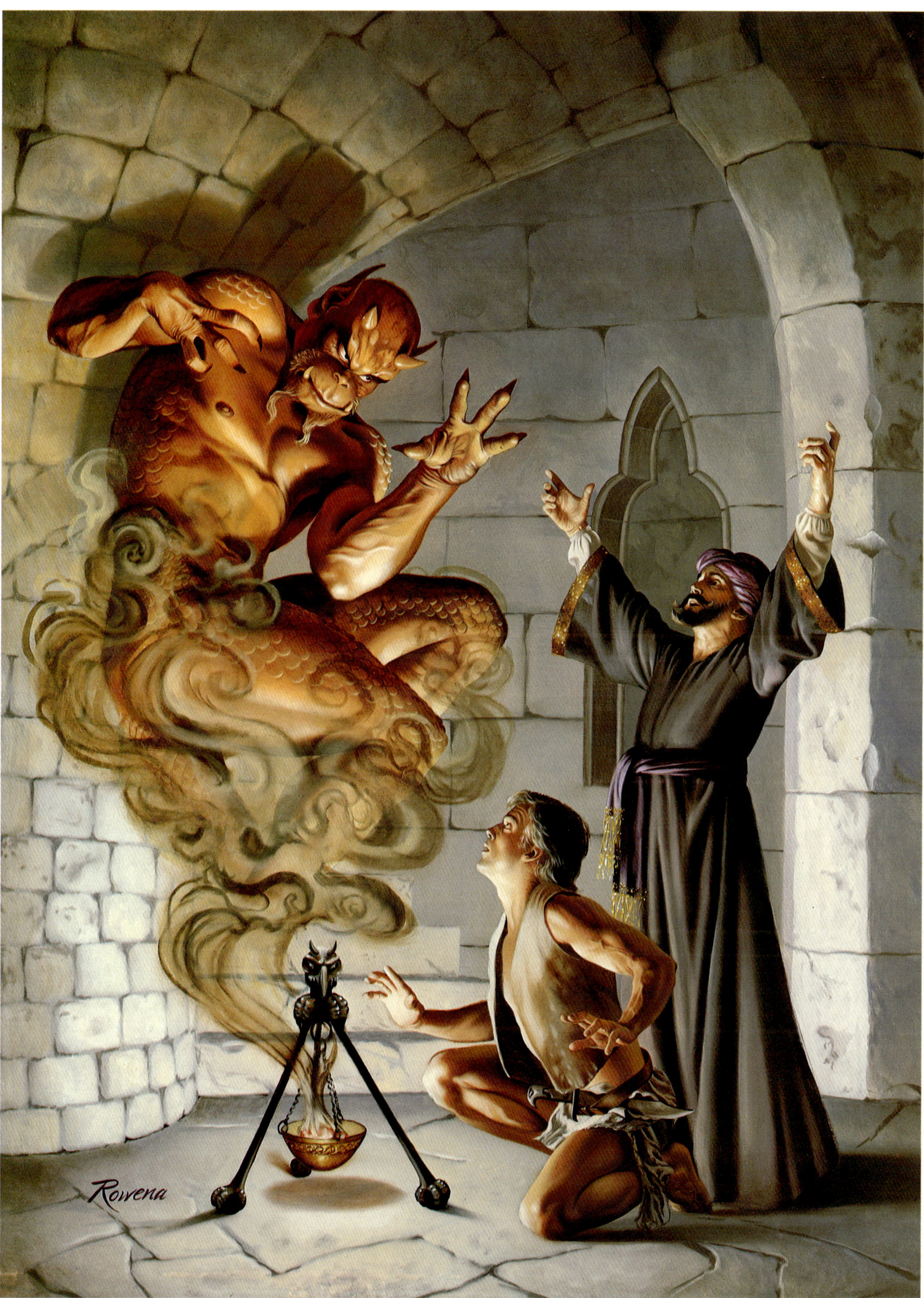
Rowena

THE DUNWICH HORROR

This was my first, bona fide monster, completely alien from head to toe, and what pleasure I had designing him! Lovecraft was a great inspiration, and I have been hooked on creatures ever since. I did most of the painting in acrylics, a tedious operation that convinced me to switch completely to oils.

(Berkley Publishing Group)

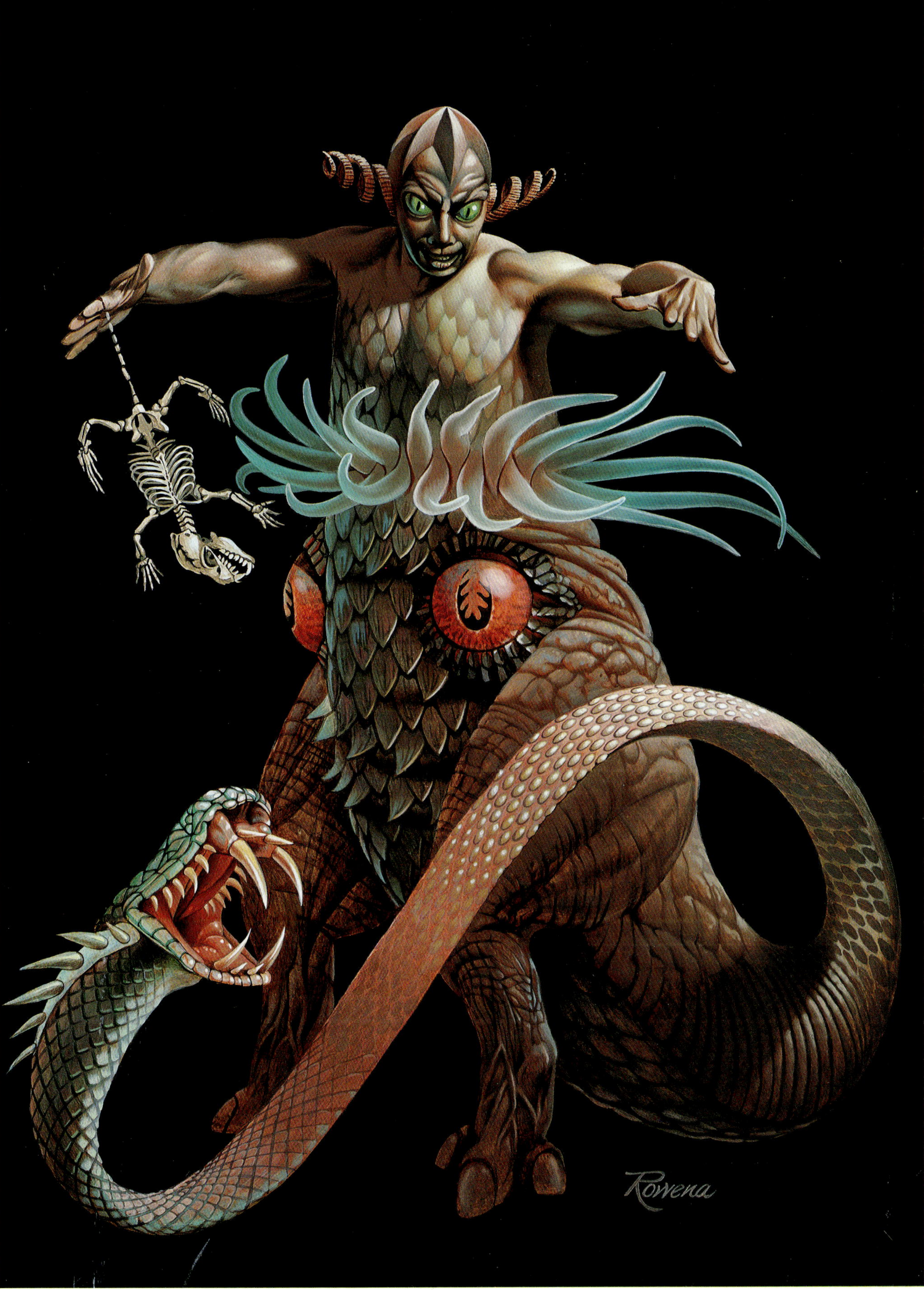
Rowena

THE WAR HOUND AND THE WORLD'S PAIN

I wanted it to look as if this devil were coming to get you.
This is another painting in which I feel
the threatening creature has a distinctly captivating side.
I personally wouldn't mind being carried off by him.

(Pocket Books)

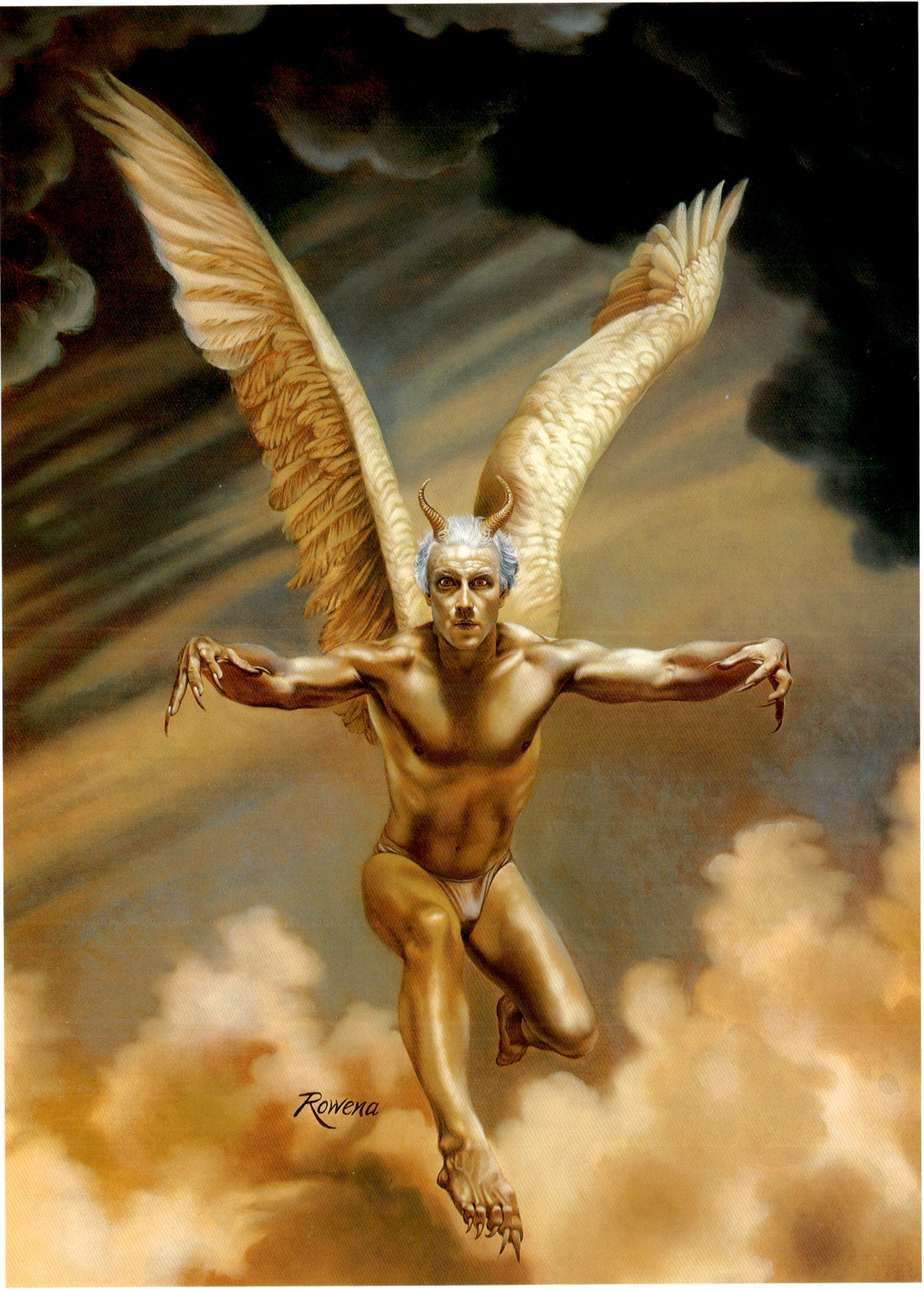
Rowena

THE LAST INCANTATION

It is always fun to do elaborate costumes in a painting, and my impulse is to use van Eyck as my inspiration and render everything to death. The deadlines for illustrations never allow me to push things to the limit; therefore, I keep producing paintings at a reasonable rate. Left to my own devices, I would labor over each piece for years.

(Timescape)

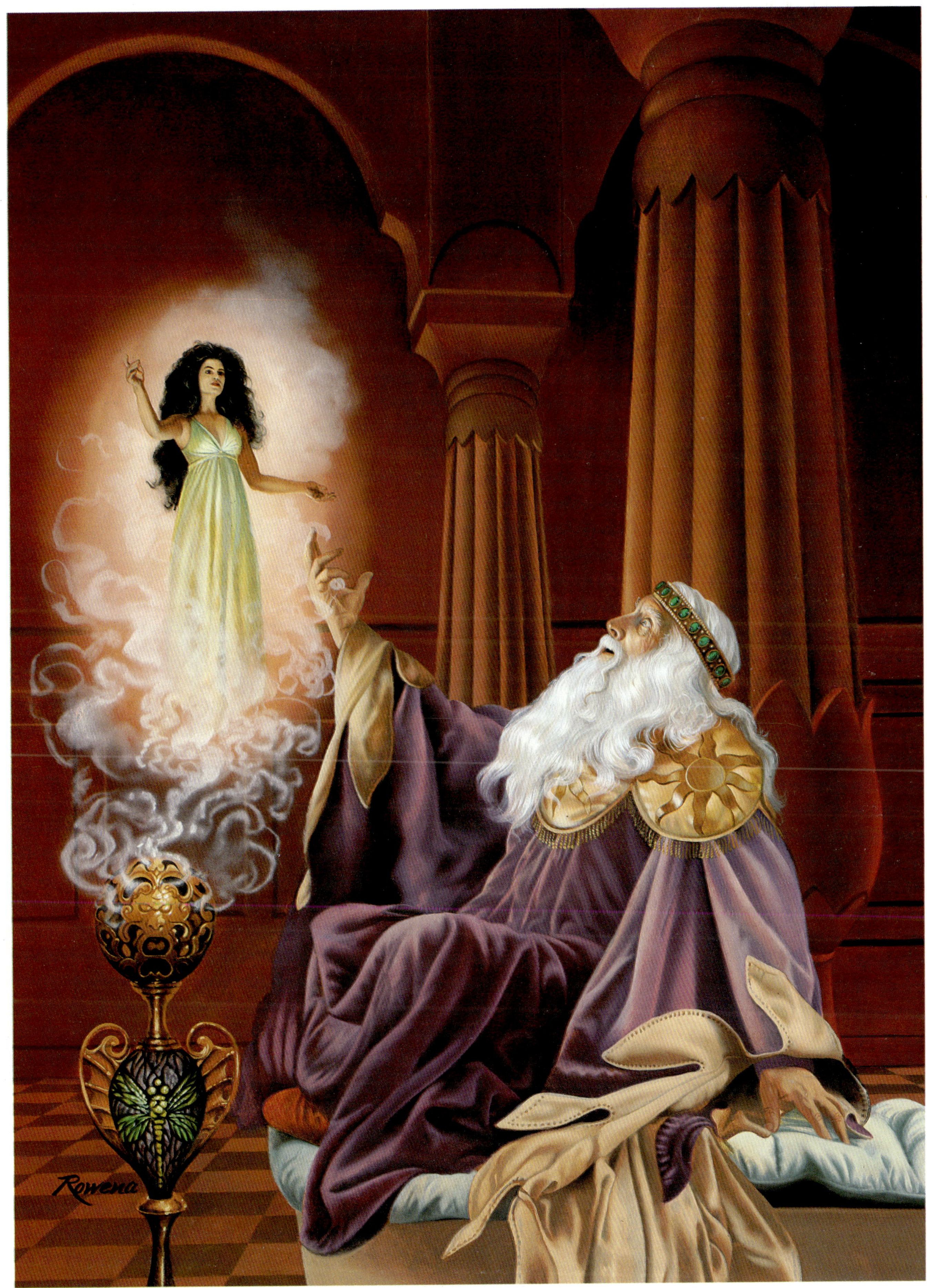
Rowena

THE DEVIL WIVES OF LI FONG

This book was just full of imagery that I like to paint,
such as action, color, and exotic characters.
Since I have a real weakness for rendering textures like silk and satin,
I enjoyed working on the man's purple jacket
and the girl's silk shirt.

(Del Ray)

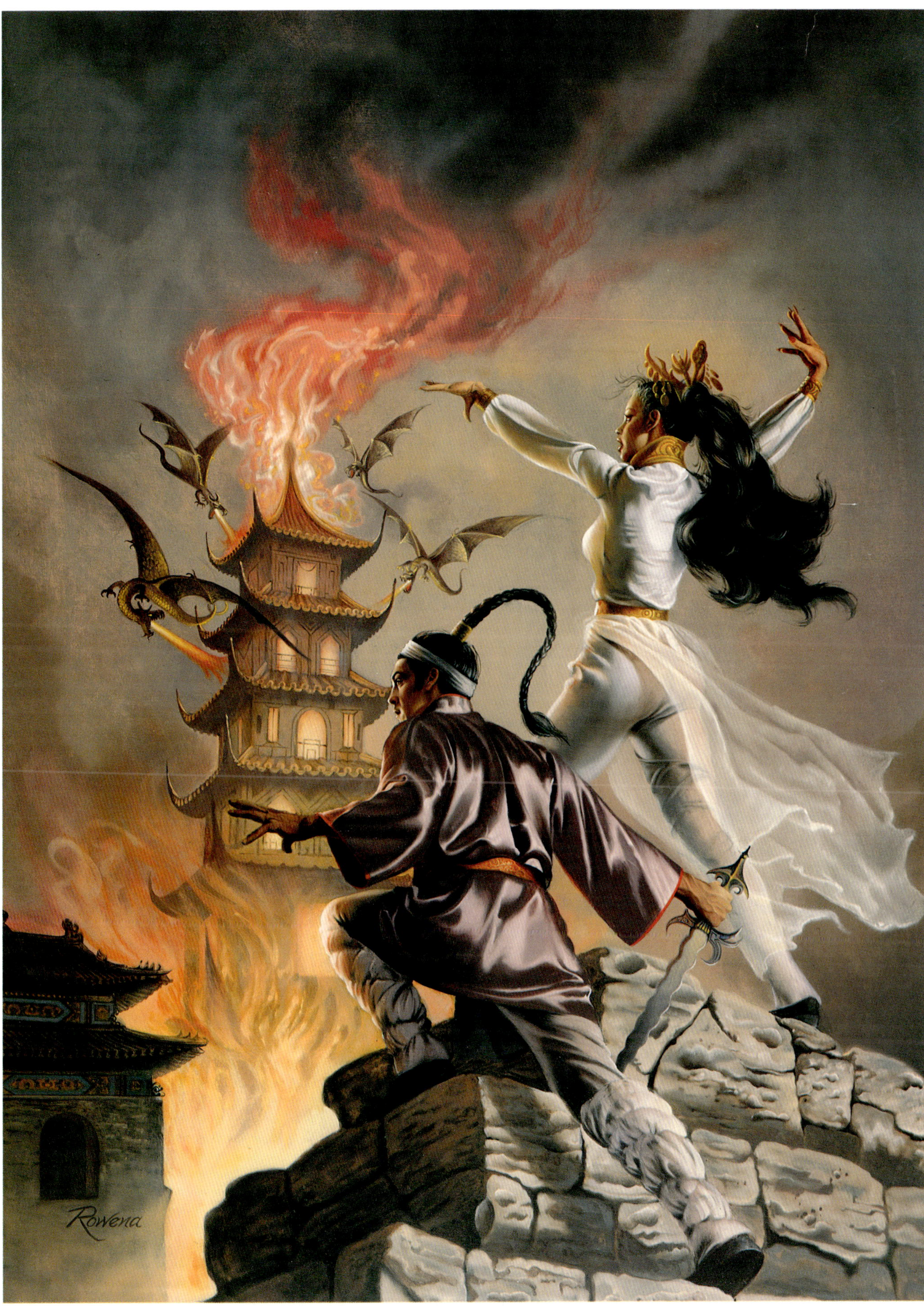
Rowena

VISION OF TAROT

I like the concept of this painting,
a wild female mounted on her ferocious monster
with a hidden observer up in a tree,
but there are several things about it I would like to change.
It is one of those learning paintings,
for which you do another one like it later that works better.

(Berkley Publishing Group)

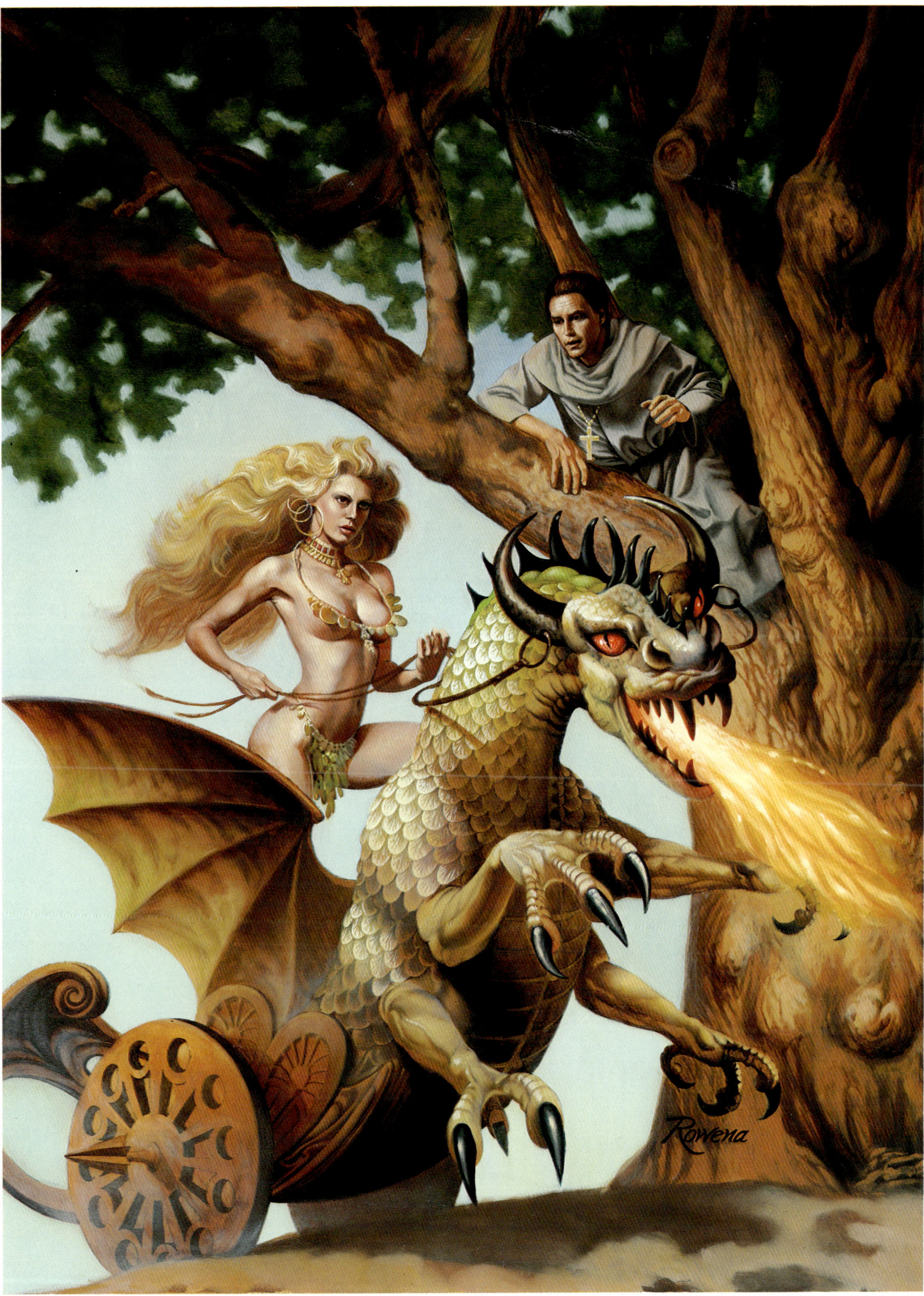
Rowena

Rowena Morrill: Artist . . .

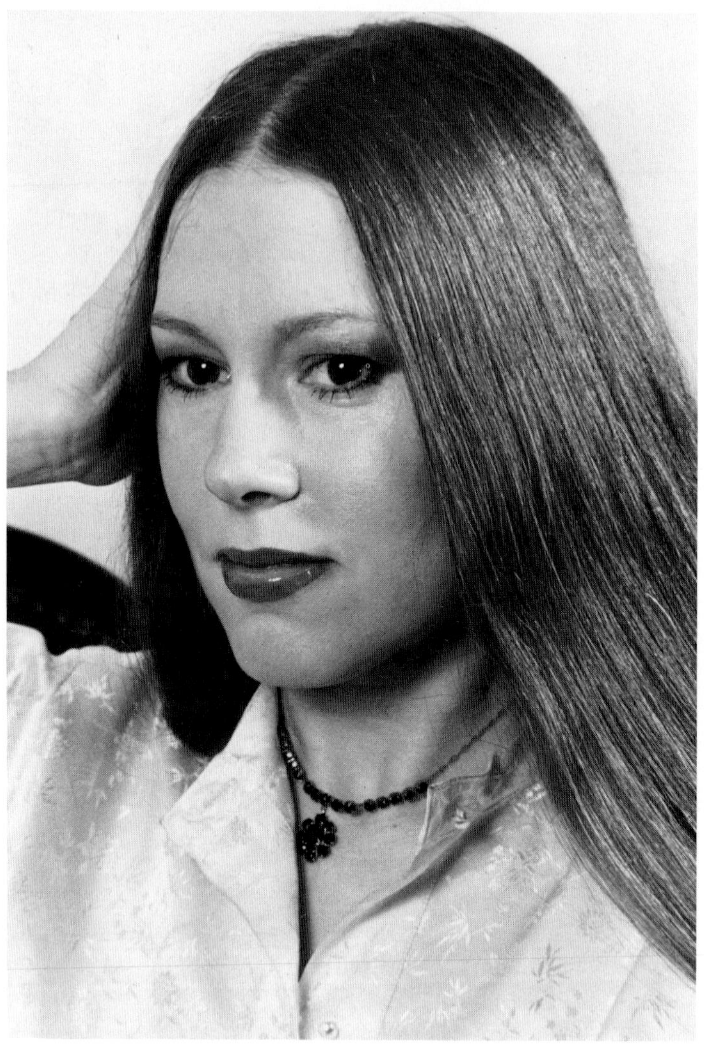

Rowena Morrill was born into a mobile military family in 1944 and had the opportunity to travel widely as a child. She absorbed a diversity of cultures in such places as Japan, Italy and many parts of the United States, to which she now attributes much of her inspiration. Rowena began painting at age twenty-three due to her restlessness as a military wife, but it wasn't long before her painting evolved from a part-time avocation to a full-time occupation. In the course of the next ten years she brought together her diverse experience, vivid imagination, inspiration and talent and developed the style and technique for which she is now so well known. Since 1975 Rowena has lived and worked in New York and has become a celebrity to science fiction fans, artists and art students. Aside from illustrating book covers for more than a dozen publishers in both the United States and Europe, she has participated in gallery and museum exhibitions throughout the country, and her work is found in important private and museum collections worldwide. Rowena Morrill is unquestionably the most significant female fantasy painter in the world today.

Printed in Switzerland